Collective Impact

Overcoming the Twelve Enemies of Teacher Efficacy

Jenni DONOHOO • Glenn FORBES

Foreword by ***Tommy Thompson***

Solution Tree | Press

Artificial intelligence outputs of micro-move summaries featured in the appendix were generated with the assistance of Claude.ai.

555 North Morton Street
Bloomington, IN 47404
800.733.6786 (toll free) / 812.336.7700
FAX: 812.336.7790

email: info@SolutionTree.com
SolutionTree.com

Visit **go.SolutionTree.com/teacherefficacy** to download the free reproducibles in this book.

Printed in the United States of America

Library of Congress Cataloging-in-Publication Data

Names: Donohoo, Jenni, author. | Forbes, Glenn, author.
Title: Collective impact : overcoming the twelve enemies of teacher efficacy / Jenni Donohoo, Glenn Forbes.
Description: Bloomington, IN : Solution Tree Press, 2025. | Includes bibliographical references and index.
Identifiers: LCCN 2024041352 (print) | LCCN 2024041353 (ebook) | ISBN 9798893740196 (paperback) | ISBN 9798893740202 (ebook)
Subjects: LCSH: Effective teaching. | Teachers--Professional relationships. | School environment.
Classification: LCC LB1025.3 .D673 2025 (print) | LCC LB1025.3 (ebook) | DDC 371.102--dc23/eng/20241203
LC record available at https://lccn.loc.gov/2024041352
LC ebook record available at https://lccn.loc.gov/2024041353

Solution Tree
Jeffrey C. Jones, CEO
Edmund M. Ackerman, President

Solution Tree Press
President and Publisher: Douglas M. Rife
Associate Publishers: Todd Brakke and Kendra Slayton
Editorial Director: Laurel Hecker
Art Director: Rian Anderson
Copy Chief: Jessi Finn
Production Editor: Paige Duke
Copy Editor: Mark Hain
Proofreader: Anne Marie Watkins
Text and Cover Designer: Rian Anderson
Acquisitions Editors: Carol Collins and Hilary Goff
Content Development Specialist: Amy Rubenstein
Associate Editors: Sarah Ludwig and Elijah Oates
Editorial Assistant: Anne Marie Watkins

Acknowledgments

The "enemies of efficacy" concept used in this book was first conceived by our friend and colleague Tommy Thompson. We'd like to acknowledge Tommy for providing the inspiration and thank him for writing the foreword to this book.

We would also like to thank Jenni's husband, Jim, for providing valuable feedback along the way. Jim's insights and suggestions helped to strengthen the manuscript, and we'd like to acknowledge him as a critical friend.

We'd like to thank the Solution Tree team for their encouragement, support, and guidance throughout the publication process.

Solution Tree Press would like to thank the following reviewers:

Justin Heinold
Principal
New Prairie High School
New Carlisle, Indiana

Jennifer Renegar
Data & Assessment Specialist
Republic School District
Republic, Missouri

Katie Saunders
Principal
Bath Community School
Bath, New Brunswick, Canada

Ringnolda Jofee' Tremain
Chief Academic Officer
East Fort Worth Montessori Academy
Fort Worth, Texas

Steven Weber
Assistant Principal
Rogers Heritage High School
Rogers, Arkansas

Visit **go.SolutionTree.com/teacherefficacy** to download the free reproducibles in this book.

Table of Contents

Chapter 11

Chapter 12

Appendix

About the Authors

Jenni Donohoo, PhD, is a professional learning facilitator, author, and researcher. Jenni has been an educator for more than twenty-five years, with experience in elementary, secondary, and postsecondary settings. She has multiyear partnerships with numerous organizations and government agencies where she works alongside system and school leaders supporting high-quality professional learning designed to improve outcomes for all students. Her areas of focus include collective teacher efficacy, collaborative inquiry, and metacognition.

Jenni is a five-time best-selling author and her books have been translated into several languages. As the director of the Jenni Donohoo Center for Collective Efficacy, she has been recognized internationally as an educational thought leader. Jenni has been a keynote speaker at conferences including WorldEduLead, Raising Student Achievement, Annual Visible Learning, Corwin's Women in Education, and the LEAP Conference in Australia.

Jenni received a bachelor of arts degree in art history and an honors bachelor of arts in sociology from the University of Windsor, and a master's degree in education from the University of Windsor. She earned a PhD in education from the joint program at the University of Windsor, Brock University, and Lakehead University, all in Ontario, Canada.

Glenn Forbes is a school principal and school improvement coach in Brisbane, Queensland, Australia. He has been an educator since 2000, moving from classroom teaching to principalship. His principal experience ranges from small, one-teacher rural schools to leading large, diverse, and complex metropolitan schools. Glenn's strong belief in cultivating collective teacher efficacy and establishing a culture of high expectations has resulted in marked improvement in various schools.

Glenn is a member of the Queensland Association of State School Principals (QASSP). He chairs the curriculum subcommittee and serves as president of the Ipswich branch. He has been the recipient of the QASSP Travelling Scholars grant, which he used to further his knowledge of the collective teacher efficacy construct. His schools have been recognized at Queensland's Showcase Awards for Excellence in Schools for excellence in parent and community engagement and excellence in early and primary-years education. Glenn has presented at the World Education Summit with Jenni Donohoo and has been a keynote speaker at several conferences. He has had several articles published in *The Queensland Principal* journal. Glenn has been a member of the Menzies School Leadership Incubator Advisory Board, which has been tasked with building a pipeline of school leaders equipped to lead and grow collective efficacy.

Glenn received his undergraduate degree in primary education and a master's degree in learning management from Central Queensland University.

Foreword

By TOMMY THOMPSON

"I wonder." Two words I associate with bestselling author and friend Jenni Donohoo. Her wondering, curiosity, *and* vulnerability started the conversation that led to this book. Jenni had just finished a keynote speech at a conference we attended. "What did you think?" she asked. I replied, "You know, Jenni, it was brilliant. But collective teacher efficacy sounds like unicorns and rainbows. As a school principal, I know there's a lot of stuff that gets in the way. I call these things the enemies of efficacy." She said, "Tell me more." And so, I did. That brief conversation between two colleagues soon led to co-presenting at conferences and ultimately this timely contribution to our noble profession.

As programs, priorities, and personnel in the ever-changing landscape of education often shift, they create a complex labyrinth for leaders to navigate. Leaders don't traverse landscapes alone, but influence others to walk with them. Part of influencing or leadership is instilling confidence in others. At the heart of teacher efficacy is the belief in one's ability to positively influence students' learning outcomes. Collective teacher efficacy extends this idea beyond the individual to the harnessed energy of a group or collective of educators who believe they can bring about positive change.

To some, beliefs and feelings are not considered as important as curriculum, instruction, and assessment. Yet, in matters of life and death, the medical field still recognizes the power of mindset. Used for centuries in medicine, a *placebo* is anything that is thought to have the active substance meant to affect health. In a recent meta-analysis, researchers reviewed ninety randomized control trials, including 9,985 adult participants and concluded that the simple yet powerful *belief* that one can be helped can have a profound positive impact (Bschor, Negel, Unger, Schwarzer, Baethge, 2024). To underestimate the power of the mind is to underestimate science. In this book, Jenni Donohoo and coauthor, Glenn Forbes, highlight what diminishes efficacy and why. They then present research that will help efficacy builders understand what people may need in a given context to strengthen their efficacy beliefs.

The sources that strengthen efficacy are known by many thanks to Albert Bandura (2006), who proposed four sources of self-efficacy: mastery experiences, vicarious experiences, persuasion, and physiological states (feelings and emotions). Too often, leaders will use a source that would strengthen their own efficacy or one that might just be easier to employ, which may be insufficient in helping others. For example, when consulting, I often poll school administrators with a series of questions to illustrate the point. First, I ask, "In most situations, when faced with a challenge, which of the four sources of efficacy would you prefer to strengthen your efficacy?" Inevitably, there are a variety of different answers and explanations justifying the responses. Next, I ask, "Which source do you often use to strengthen the efficacy of those you serve?" Nearly 100 percent of the time, leaders point to persuasion, whether at staff meetings or through email. This leads to the last question, "If you recognize what you would need to strengthen your efficacy and know that what is needed varies by individual, why predominantly rely on one source?" Leaders learn through this brief exchange that efficacy builders must give those they serve what they need.

In this book, Jenni and Glenn offer twelve enemies of efficacy. This dirty dozen commonly make their way into schools and organizations. Important to note for each individual in the school, the cause of diminishing efficacy may vary. This book helps us identify and understand the enemies of efficacy but more importantly, how to overcome them. Practical solutions to combat each of the enemies of efficacy through what the authors refer to as micro-moves separate this work from others. Too often, theories or opinions are advanced without possible solutions. Glenn, a school principal for nearly two decades, brings his acute awareness of life in today's schools. Undoubtedly, he has implemented many of the micro-moves in his own school. Together, he and Jenni, with her extensive experiences in partnering with schools across the globe, offer simple and powerful actions leaders can take to strengthen efficacy.

Such insight is overdue, and yet right on time. To understand school improvement is to understand people. Effective leaders understand that the enemies of efficacy might not be our fault, but they are our problem. Herein, Jenni and Glenn bring the enemies of efficacy to light, help us understand them, and offer a path forward.

Introduction

To improve outcomes in schools, educators must believe they are capable of meeting underperforming or disadvantaged students' needs in ways that will result in better performance and increased achievement. This is the notion of collective efficacy. *Collective efficacy* is the shared conviction that educators make a significant contribution in raising student achievement despite other factors in students' lives that might pose challenges to their success. Schools with firmly established collective efficacy have higher academic achievement (Hattie, 2023). It is a powerful belief system that creates more successful outcomes in schools because collective efficacy positively impacts teachers' motivations, goals, and efforts. Educational psychologist and preeminent source on collective teacher efficacy Albert Bandura (2000) concludes that those who have a strong sense of efficacy think more strategically, put forth greater effort, and show greater commitment toward their goals.

Efficacy beliefs, or future-oriented beliefs based on past experiences, vary from one school to another (Bandura, 1998). Unfortunately, collective efficacy is often lacking in places where it's most needed. In some schools, the predominant narrative is, "No matter what we do, it won't matter. We can't reach these students. There is nothing left to try." When efficacy is lacking, teachers tend to give up more easily because they don't believe their efforts will lead to success. Bandura (2000) explains that when faced with obstacles, those who doubt their capabilities slacken their efforts, lower their goals, and settle for mediocre solutions.

Efficacy beliefs are not static, however, and can be influenced by a variety of factors. District and school leaders can intentionally foster a sense of collective teacher efficacy. This book provides strategies for doing so. An effective efficacy builder must know how to tap into the sources of efficacy. They need an awareness of how to create the conditions that foster it at high levels. Finally, they need a strategic approach in combating the enemies of efficacy. This book provides the clarity, strategy, and guidance to do just that.

How Efficacy Beliefs Are Formed and Why Collective Efficacy Is Important

There are four sources that influence individual and collective efficacy (Bandura, 1998).

1. **Mastery experiences:** The most potent source of efficacy-shaping information for teachers is collaborative success on a challenging task, called *mastery experiences*. Mastery experiences strengthen efficacy when teachers interpret success through a growth mindset. Efficacy increases when teachers make a direct link between their combined efforts and resulting positive outcomes.
2. **Vicarious experiences:** Efficacy is also enhanced when teachers see others like themselves succeed.
3. **Persuasion:** The third source comes in the form of both verbal and social persuasion. When a credible and trustworthy colleague convinces a teacher or team that they have what it takes to succeed, it can foster a greater sense of efficacy. Also, when people are influenced by their environments and interactions with others, it can influence efficacy.
4. **Feelings and emotions:** The last mode of influence is what psychologists refer to as physiological or affective states. *Affective states* are feelings and emotions that can be positive or negative. For example, positive feelings include delight, excitement, and joy, while negative emotions include confusion, frustration, and anxiety. Positive feelings boost efficacy and negative feelings diminish it.

According to John Hattie's (2023) Visible Learning synthesis, collective teacher efficacy is the number-one factor in raising student achievement, with an effect size of 1.34.

The ways that efficacy beliefs influence thoughts, feelings, motivations, and behaviors help to explain why they make such a difference in learning and teaching. Research demonstrates several productive effects of collective teacher efficacy, including increased student achievement (Hattie,

2023), reduction in inequity (Goddard, Skrla, & Salloum, 2017), increased teacher professional satisfaction (Klassen, Usher, & Bong, 2010), and deeper levels of implementation of evidence-based strategies (Donohoo & Katz, 2020). Let's look at a few others in more detail.

- **Is cost effective:** Collective efficacy is not a costly program or an initiative. It does not come prepackaged in a box or a kit. It is a mindset that influences how educators think, feel, motivate themselves, and behave (Bandura, 2000).
- **Promotes positivity:** Bandura (2000) notes that efficacy beliefs "influence whether people think erratically or strategically; optimistically or pessimistically" (p. 75). In schools where efficacy is developed, educators think passionately about their work and value opportunities for professional learning. They show greater academic optimism (Vanlommel, van den Boom-Muilenburg, Thesingh, & Kikken, 2023) and are less prone to pessimism (Parker, 1994).
- **Supports job satisfaction:** Collective efficacy influences how educators feel when faced with challenging circumstances. A strong sense of efficacy helps make educators less vulnerable to the discouragement that can overcome teams when taking on tough problems (Bandura, 2000). Studies show that collective efficacy beliefs are a main determinant of teachers' job satisfaction (Caprara, Barbaranelli, Borgogni, & Steca, 2003; Klassen et al., 2010; Yurt, 2022). Efficacy beliefs also determine how much stress educators experience when coping with the taxing demands of the profession.
- **Creates motivation:** Collective efficacy influences how educators motivate themselves to realize greater collective impact. It's been demonstrated to have a positive and significant impact on student achievement (Bandura, 1993; Goddard, Hoy, & Hoy, 2000; Salloum, 2021). Collective efficacy helps determine how much effort educators put into team endeavors along with the goals they set. A strong sense of efficacy results in higher goals and firmer commitments to them (Bandura, 1998).
- **Encourages perseverance:** Finally, collective efficacy also influences how educators behave when faced with difficult circumstances. A strong sense of efficacy results in the staying power needed when collective efforts fail to produce quick results. Efficacious teams make better use of resources and find ways to make evidence-based approaches work in their unique environments (Donohoo & Katz, 2020). Furthermore, Wayne K. Hoy, C. John Tarter, and Anita Woolfolk Hoy (2006) write that an emphasis on

> academics captures the behavioral enactment of efficacy. In other words, when teachers put a lot of effort into academic work with their students, it's a visible sign they believe in their ability to make a difference. They're actively demonstrating their collective efficacy through their focus on academics.

Imagine what could be possible if everyone in an educational setting believed, individually and collectively, that they had the capability to achieve positive results. Visualize the wide-ranging possibilities in schools where efficacy is developed. A strong sense of efficacy helps schools generate the focus, commitment, and action they need to address their current challenges. Collective efficacy makes possible the collaboration and collective impact we need to create a more fulfilling, equitable, and transformative education system for today's generation and future generations. Collective efficacy creates results over excuses.

Leading schools is complex work. Principals attempting this work alone are unlikely to succeed. Without a strategic approach, well-meaning teams will likely also fall short of realizing their potential. The key to achieving success is harnessing the power of collective efficacy to achieve collective impact. *Collective impact* is achieved through high levels of collective efficacy. When school teams *really believe* that all students can achieve their potential, then great things can happen. Improving one teacher, one class, or one school at a time is too slow. To fulfill the promise of an equitable educational system for all, we must mobilize the collective by cultivating strong systems of belief. This is collective efficacy in action.

The Enemies of Efficacy

In this book, we identify twelve "enemies of efficacy"—a phrase coined by our friend and colleague Tommy Thompson. Consider the twelve enemies, which pose a direct threat to individual and collective efficacy.

1. Blame
2. Magnitude
3. Compliance
4. Negativity
5. Judgment
6. Uncertainty
7. Avoidance
8. Comparison
9. Hierarchy
10. Isolation
11. Ambiguity
12. Fragmentation

To extend the personification of the enemies of efficacy metaphor, we further perceive these enemies as trying to do damage and actively oppose the development of efficacy.

Table I.1 outlines the differences in schools characterized by a strong sense of efficacy compared to those where efficacy is weak. The characteristics of a weakened sense of efficacy (shown in the right column) comprise the twelve enemies of efficacy that you will learn more about in this book.

Table I.1: Where Efficacy Is Strong and Where It Is Weak

A Strong Sense of Collective Efficacy	A Weakened Sense of Collective Efficacy
Feedback culture	Blame game
Perspective taking	Overwhelmed by magnitude
Commitment to learning	Compliance crushes creativity
Genuine positivity	Dominated by a negative narrative
Psychological safety	Judgment stifles joint work
Greater well-being	Uncertainty causes undue stress
Action oriented	Avoidance oriented
Improvement based on criteria	Social comparison
Teachers feel empowered	Hierarchical structures limit problem solving
Task and goal interdependence	Feelings of isolation
Consensus among team members	Ambiguity about what's important
Focus is well defined	Fragmentation due to initiative overload

System and school leaders can make a concerted effort to overcome these enemies. In this book, you'll encounter practical strategies for doing so. For each enemy of efficacy, you will find three strategies you can use to stop that enemy from sabotaging the path to success.

Theory of Action

To effectively implement these strategies and create lasting improvement, leaders can employ a *theory of action*: a structured approach that links specific interventions to desired outcomes in overcoming the enemies of efficacy. A theory of action outlines how specific actions or strategies are expected to lead to desired outcomes. It's essentially a road map that connects what you do (your actions) to what you want to achieve (your goals). The following twelve statements capture our theory of action for overcoming the enemies of efficacy. The overarching leadership actions in bold in each of the sentences are proven practices for driving meaningful improvement in schools and overcoming the enemies of efficacy, shown in italics. Even if the focus is not on strengthening collective efficacy in schools, by prioritizing these leadership actions, principals will develop the capacity to lead successful and sustainable improvement. As an additional benefit, by utilizing these moves, leaders enhance collective efficacy, which has a strong correlation to increased student achievement.

1. By **giving effective feedback**, school leaders can overcome *blame* as an enemy of efficacy.
2. By **framing challenges appropriately**, school leaders can overcome *magnitude* as an enemy of efficacy.
3. By **garnering commitment**, school leaders can overcome *compliance* as an enemy of efficacy.
4. By **elevating positivity**, school leaders can overcome *negativity* as an enemy of efficacy.
5. By **enhancing psychological safety**, school leaders can overcome *judgment* as an enemy of efficacy.
6. By **prioritizing well-being**, school leaders can overcome *uncertainty* as an enemy of efficacy.
7. By **embedding reflection into teachers' daily routines**, school leaders can overcome *avoidance* as an enemy of efficacy.
8. By **measuring progress against a predetermined criterion**, school leaders can overcome *comparison* as an enemy of efficacy.
9. By **developing teacher leaders**, school leaders can overcome *hierarchy* as an enemy of efficacy.
10. By **increasing interdependencies**, school leaders can overcome *isolation* as an enemy of efficacy.
11. By **building consensus**, school leaders can overcome *ambiguity* as an enemy of efficacy.
12. By **focusing on implementation**, school leaders can overcome *fragmentation* as an enemy of efficacy.

This book has two aims. The first is to help build further awareness of collective efficacy, what it is, and why it matters. The second is to help bridge the gap between theory and practice by providing practical ideas for principals to strengthen efficacy in schools. By identifying potential enemies of efficacy, system and school leaders can apply micro-moves to overcome barriers that prevent efficacy from developing. *Micro-moves* are small steps leaders can take to engage teachers meaningfully and respectfully in school improvement. In a study that examines how leaders learn, Steven Katz (2015) notes that micro-moves are easier to track and learn from: "Larger moves were very difficult to monitor because you end up not knowing which part of the move worked or didn't" (p. 6). These small moves are consequential in generating the momentum and enthusiasm needed to realize collective efficacy and impact.

As we share the micro-moves that principals can use to overcome the enemies of efficacy, we will make explicit links to the sources of efficacy and point out ways in which principals can intentionally shape these types of experiences in schools.

Table I.2 (page 8) provides an overview of the micro-moves school principals can use to overcome each enemy of efficacy.

How to Use This Book

As table I.2 (page 8) illustrates, this book is divided into four parts—one for each of the sources of efficacy. We encourage you *not* to read this book straight through. Review the four parts and the table of contents and identify the enemies of efficacy that most resonate with you based on your school context. What do your instincts and your observations tell you about which enemies might be present in your school? Start there. Each chapter includes a description of the enemy of efficacy and three micro-moves you can employ to overcome the enemy. The chapters are short by design. At the end of each chapter, you'll find reflection questions and exercises you can use to contextualize the information and support transfer to practice.

It is important to understand how individuals and teams interpret what they are capable of accomplishing to support the development of efficacy. Therefore, we will revisit the sources of collective efficacy to introduce each of the four parts of this book. This background information will help you better understand the theoretical foundations for overcoming the enemies of efficacy. We also highlight explicit links about how school leaders can tap into these sources of efficacy in featured areas entitled "Tapping Into the Sources of Efficacy."

Part 1 illustrates how persuasion functions as one of the four sources of efficacy.

Table 1.2. Micro-Moves for Overcoming the Enemies of Efficacy

Part 1: Persuasion		
Chapter 1: Feedback Over Blame • Normalizing Coaching Feedback • Emphasizing the Role of Effort and Strategy Use • Providing Frequent Updating	**Chapter 2: Perspective Over Magnitude** • Framing Through Emphasizing and De-Emphasizing • Framing Different Futures • Framing Challenges Into Smaller Pieces	**Chapter 3: Commitment Over Compliance** • Highlighting a Gap • Learning From Marker Students • Surfacing the Cost of Inaction
Part 2: Positive Emotions		
Chapter 4: Positivity Over Negativity • Labeling Emotions • Recognizing and Celebrating Progress • Leveraging the Power of the Narrative	**Chapter 5: Psychological Safety Over Judgment** • Understanding Different Ways of Communicating • Modeling the Norms of Collaboration • Sharing Feedback	**Chapter 6: Well-Being Over Uncertainty** • Building Workplace Well-Being Profiles • Addressing Teachers' Concerns • Increasing Interpersonal Clarity
Part 3: Mastery Experiences		
Chapter 7: Action Over Avoidance • Posing Reflective Questions • Modeling Evidence-Based Reflection • Guiding Strengths-Based Approaches	**Chapter 8: Criteria Over Comparison** • Setting Mastery Goals • Identifying Criterion-Based Success • Providing Goal-Referenced Feedback	**Chapter 9: Empowerment Over Hierarchy** • Validating Informal Leadership • Expanding Opportunities for Formal Leadership • Increasing Teacher Autonomy and Decision-Making Power
Part 4: Vicarious Experiences		
Chapter 10: Interdependence Over Isolation • Extending Invitations to Say More • Helping Teams Set Interdependent Goals • Engaging Teams in Interdependent Tasks	**Chapter 11: Consensus Over Ambiguity** • Guiding an Affinity-Mapping Process • Using the Realm of Concern Versus Realm of Influence Protocol • Analyzing Student Work Samples	**Chapter 12: Focus Over Fragmentation** • Gatekeeping • Applying the 80/20 Principle • Prioritizing Evidence-Based Strategies

In chapter 1, we explore how feedback can overcome blame as an enemy of efficacy using three micro-moves: normalizing coaching feedback, emphasizing the role of effort and strategy use, and providing frequent updating. In chapter 2, we show how framing challenges appropriately can overcome magnitude as an enemy of efficacy with the help of three micro-moves: framing through emphasizing and de-emphasizing, framing different futures, and framing challenges into smaller pieces. In chapter 3, we examine how garnering commitment can overcome compliance as an enemy of efficacy when leaders employ three micro-moves: highlighting a gap, learning from marker students, and surfacing the cost of inaction.

Part 2 explores how positive emotions enhance efficacy.

In chapter 4, we show that elevating positivity can overcome negativity as an enemy of efficacy using three micro-moves: labeling emotions, recognizing and celebrating progress, and leveraging the power of the narrative. In chapter 5, we illustrate how enhancing psychological safety can overcome judgment as an enemy of efficacy when leaders practice three micro-moves: understanding different ways of communicating, modeling the norms of collaboration, and sharing feedback. In chapter 6, we explore how prioritizing well-being can overcome uncertainty as an enemy of efficacy with the help of three micro-moves: building workplace well-being profiles, addressing teachers' concerns, and increasing interpersonal clarity.

Part 3 names mastery experiences as the most potent source of collective efficacy.

In chapter 7, we note that embedding reflection into teachers' daily routines can overcome avoidance as an enemy of efficacy using three micro-moves: posing reflective questions, modeling evidence-based reflection, and guiding strengths-based approaches. In chapter 8, we examine how measuring progress against a predetermined criterion can overcome comparison as an enemy of efficacy with the help of three micro-moves: setting mastery goals, identifying success criteria, and providing goal-referenced feedback. In chapter 9, we explore how developing teacher leaders can overcome hierarchy as an enemy of efficacy when leaders employ three micro-moves: validating informal leadership, expanding opportunities for formal teacher leadership, and increasing teacher autonomy and decision-making power.

Part 4 discusses how vicarious experiences are a powerful source of collective efficacy.

In chapter 10, we note that increasing interdependencies can overcome isolation as an enemy of efficacy with the help of three micro-moves: extending invitations to say more, helping teams set interdependent goals, and engaging teams in interdependent tasks. In chapter 11, we look at building consensus to overcome ambiguity as an enemy of efficacy by employing three micro-moves: guiding an affinity-mapping process, using the realm of concern and the realm of influence, and analyzing student work samples. In chapter 12, we explore how focusing on implementation can overcome fragmentation as an enemy of efficacy using three micro-moves: gatekeeping, applying the 80/20 principle, and prioritizing evidence-based strategies.

As we explore how to overcome the enemies of efficacy, remember that each micro-move can lead to significant improvement. In the following chapters, we'll explore practical strategies to build a culture of collective efficacy in your school, starting with persuasive techniques that school leaders can use to initiate change.

Part 1

Persuasion

As you read in the introduction, Bandura (2006) identifies persuasion as one of the four sources of efficacy. Persuasion is about encouraging, prompting, and influencing others to engage in the actions needed to bring about continuous school improvement. Principals play an instrumental role in persuading teachers to actively participate in improvement initiatives. School leaders are key influencers who can create the conditions for teachers to build collective efficacy and embrace change.

Bandura (1998) notes that there are "distinctive sets of factors that can affect persuasory efficacy information" (p. 55). These include credibility, expertise, and trustworthiness. Ultimately, the success of a school leader's persuasive efforts lies in their ability to establish credibility, demonstrate commitment to continuous learning, and build trust. By leveraging these key factors, the principal can foster a culture of trust, learning, and continuous improvement, leading to better outcomes for both teachers and students. Let's take a closer look at each of these factors.

- **Credibility:** Principals are considered credible when they demonstrate an understanding of evidence-based practices, current research, and the unique challenges their school community faces.
- **Expertise:** We prefer to think of an expert as a lifelong learner rather than someone who has all the answers. When principals are committed to continuous learning, they model the importance of continuous growth and demonstrate that they can adapt to the often-changing landscape of education.
- **Trustworthiness:** Perhaps most importantly, a principal must build trust with their teachers by being transparent, consistent, and supportive.

In chapters 1 through 3, we identify three enemies of efficacy and draw on two types of persuasion—verbal persuasion and social persuasion—to overcome these enemies. Through verbal persuasion, leaders focus on using language to influence teachers and tap into various social influences that can shape individuals' and teams' attitudes, beliefs, and behaviors. A principal can effectively persuade teachers by strategically using feedback, framing challenges appropriately, and sparking a sense of purpose.

In part 1, we discuss the following micro-moves.

- By *normalizing coaching feedback* and making it a more frequent occurrence, principals can influence how teachers use feedback to improve teaching and learning.
- By *emphasizing the role of effort and strategy use*, principals can foster growth mindsets and minimize attributional biases.
- By *providing frequent updating* through the sharing of information, principals can help teachers in revising their thinking based on current data and evidence.
- By *framing through emphasizing and de-emphasizing*, principals can change the way teachers perceive challenges.
- By *framing different futures*, principals can help teachers think differently about student trajectories.
- By *framing challenges into smaller pieces*, principals can help educators feel less overwhelmed.
- By *highlighting a gap*, principals can make teachers aware of inequities and spark a sense of purpose to meet the needs of all students.
- By *learning from marker students*, principals can help teachers solve contextual issues related to students' unique needs.
- Finally, by *surfacing the cost of inaction*, principals create a sense of urgency and motivation for change.

Chapter 1

Feedback Over Blame

Through *effective feedback,* school leaders can overcome *blame* as an enemy of efficacy.

In this chapter, we discover how blame functions as an enemy of efficacy. Fortunately, feedback operates as a tool for school leaders to overcome blame and enhance collective efficacy among educators. Three key micro-moves for providing efficacy-enhancing feedback include normalizing coaching feedback, emphasizing the role of effort and strategy use, and providing frequent updating. School leaders achieve collective impact as they overcome blame through feedback.

Blame as an Enemy of Efficacy

In the introduction (page 1), you learned that efficacy beliefs result from thoughts that individuals have about themselves and others regarding their ability to perform the tasks and responsibilities necessary to improve student outcomes. Inherent in this definition is a cause-and-effect relationship: teaching causes learning. What the adults in school buildings do directly impacts the students in their care. Consider the following examples.

- By engaging students in rehearsal, teachers can increase students' retention of concepts.
- Educators can use restorative practices to increase respect among students, their peers, and the teaching faculty.
- By utilizing anticipatory activities, teachers help students to activate prior knowledge.
- By engaging students in deliberate practice, teachers can help to increase their skills.

Individual and collective efficacy recognizes that educators make a difference through their ongoing efforts and by selecting and utilizing effective teaching and learning strategies. Remember that collective efficacy is strengthened when teachers and teams achieve success and recognize that their effort and strategies paid off. School principals can strengthen efficacy by providing feedback about effective strategies that positively impact student learning. Leaders can use persuasion to help teachers make the cause-and-effect relationship clearer.

Sometimes, however, educators attribute the effect of student success or failure to causes that are outside their realm of influence. This is especially true in schools facing significant challenges. Where there is a lack of success, there is also an innate tendency to place blame on external sources, looking outward rather than inward. For example, "The students didn't do well this year because of the communities where they come from" or "The poor outcomes on the state test were a direct result of students who don't care, don't show up, or don't have parental support." Psychologists refer to this as an *attribution bias*. In some schools, cultural norms and everyday discourse reinforce attribution bias. Placing blame on external circumstances removes educators' perception of their own failure and helps protect their professional identity.

Researchers Avner Cohen-Zamir and Dana Vedder-Weiss (2024) studied teachers' tendency to attribute blame for students' difficulties and failures to others. Consider their findings.

- Teachers blamed the students themselves (for example, "He is a very weak student") 53.5 percent of the time.
- Teachers blamed parents 19.4 percent of the time (for example, "There is no one to talk with at home").
- Teachers blamed other teachers (for example, "He wasn't well prepared in the previous grade") 17.2 percent of the time.
- Teachers blamed the education system or school management 4.1 percent of the time.
- Teachers blamed other factors 5.8 percent of the time.

It's damaging to collective efficacy when school teams blame each other or the system when things go wrong (for example, "Some departments just don't enforce the rules" or "Central office is expecting too much"). This deficit mindset can create a divide, causing an us-versus-them mentality. While the attribution bias might cause temporary relief, it hinders long-term development and growth. Furthermore, when in-fighting erodes trust, collective efficacy becomes more difficult to achieve. In schools and districts where the wisdom and benefits of recognizing and learning from failures do not exist, blame becomes more prevalent. In this respect, blame is an enemy of efficacy.

Research demonstrates that factors outside of educators' control do have some influence on student outcomes. For example, Hattie's (2023) synthesis of factors related to student achievement demonstrates that socioeconomic status had an effect size of 0.56 and home environment had an effect size of 0.40. We are not here to argue that these things do not matter. There is, however, a wealth of evidence that demonstrates that what educators think and do matters a lot more. Numerous research studies (Bandura, 1993; Goddard, Goddard, Kim, & Miller, 2015; Goddard et al., 2017; Ramos, Silva, Pontes, Fernandez, & Nina, 2014; Sandoval, Challoo, & Kupczynski, 2011) demonstrate that schools that have a firmly established sense of collective efficacy (and are otherwise similar) have higher student achievement. As noted earlier, collective teacher efficacy is at the top of Hattie's (2023) list of factors that influence student achievement.

To realize systemic and sustainable improvement in schools, principals can create and reinforce cultures that counteract the blame game. Leaders can use persuasion to help teachers better understand the impact of their efforts and become more comfortable surfacing mistakes so they can learn from them. It's in these environments where giving and receiving helpful feedback leads to learning and growth. System and school leaders can take intentional steps to overcome blame as an enemy of efficacy.

Overcome Blame With Feedback

School principals can counteract the blame game and strengthen collective efficacy by providing feedback. By normalizing feedback and making it a more purposeful occurrence, school leaders can influence how teachers think about blame and ultimately impact how teachers act on feedback to improve their practice and recognize the impact of their efforts. Principals can use feedback strategically to minimize the attribution bias within their school community.

There are many different types of feedback with varying degrees of impact. Education researchers Benedikt Wisniewski, Klaus Zierer, and John Hattie (2020) indicate there is significant variability in the effect of feedback and that its impact is substantially influenced by a variety of factors, including the information conveyed.

Feedback from principals to teachers can serve several purposes, including enhancing efficacy. Research demonstrates that "different types of feedback provided key paths for teachers to better understand their own developing teaching performance and that of other teachers" (Akkuzu, 2014, p. 37). Three micro-moves for providing efficacy-enhancing feedback include (1) normalizing coaching feedback, (2) emphasizing the role of effort and strategy use, and (3) providing frequent updating.

Normalizing Coaching Feedback

Feedback can help change us for the better or it can feel like a threat to our security. Educators Douglas Stone and Jenn David-Lang (2017) write that "feedback is fraught and complex because human relationships are fraught and complex" (p. 47). They distinguish between evaluation feedback and coaching feedback. *Evaluation feedback* often provides a judgment or rating and is focused on the outcomes or the results achieved. *Coaching feedback*, on the other hand, aims to help teachers and teams improve their performance and is focused on the processes, behaviors, and strategies that are used to achieve goals.

Stone and David-Lang (2017) suggest that disentangling coaching feedback from evaluation feedback allows "the coaching conversation to be what it's intended to be: a space to brainstorm, learn, try on ideas, share vulnerabilities, and celebrate triumphs" (p. 48). Principals can build efficacy by providing coaching feedback and normalizing it so that it is well received and becomes an everyday occurrence. Leaders must separate performance feedback (evaluation based) from process and personal feedback (coaching based).

When feedback is focused only on evaluating performance, it narrows the parameters to two choices: either achieving or not achieving success. Evaluation-style feedback based on a performance target can mentally limit a school's view of progress. A school team that demonstrates promising signs of improvement only to fall short on a performance target could experience a setback if this was the only view of success.

The way leaders *deliver* feedback is also important. Researchers Marcus Buckingham and Ashley Goodall (2019) write, "telling people what we think of their performance doesn't help them thrive and excel, and telling people how we think they should improve actually *hinders* learning" (p. 5). Therefore, leaders must be cognizant of the way in which they deliver performance feedback. When feedback is handled poorly, schools can start the blame game by shining the spotlight on the *failed* result rather than the many positive steps made in the process.

This is not to say that we shy away from discussing performance outcomes, as they are an inevitable aspect of school systems. We recognize schools should have an awareness of their performance against their goals; however, giving dedicated time and space to *separate* coaching feedback is important.

Coaching feedback, unlike evaluation feedback, which is often either-or, focuses more precisely on the people and processes. This subtle but important distinction is the very key to unlock the power of feedback in cultivating collective efficacy. When principals focus feedback on the positive way the team has engaged in an effective process, they tap into important sources of efficacy-inducing information. A micro-move is to highlight all the smaller successes achieved, even if the overall result wasn't accomplished.

To highlight this micro-move, we draw on a fictional example. After a few years of inconsistent progress, a school principal was challenged by the district superintendent to raise the English grades for their elementary students by 10 percent over the coming year. Note: we recognize how arbitrary this sounds, but this is the reality for many school principals.

The principal took up the challenge with her leadership team and redesigned a multifaceted improvement strategy that included a lesson planning protocol with clearly articulated learning intentions, success criteria, and strategies for differentiating instruction. The school team worked diligently throughout the year to rigorously implement their strategies and made some impressive gains. Ultimately, they didn't reach the target the school district set for them. In the subsequent meeting with the superintendent, the principal recounted the feedback she received. The feedback focused exclusively on the performance outcomes and how the team fell short of the target (3.6 percent gain instead of 10 percent). The principal left the meeting feeling a range of complex emotions including discouragement and self-doubt.

Having worked through this experience, the principal elected a different approach with her senior leadership team by delivering coaching-focused feedback. She shared the following observations:

> I've noticed that most of you have been very consistent in using the new lesson planning protocol we introduced this year. The way many of you break down the standards and engage students in meaningful ways with the success criteria is exemplary. It's clear that this level of intentional planning is having a positive impact on student learning.

Next, the principal worked through a reflective process with the team to explore what they felt worked well, what they could have adjusted, and next steps they could take. She also asked them to consider the degree to which they implemented the strategies in their individual classrooms. They discussed what to stop doing, what to start doing, and what they should continue doing. She ended the meeting by summarizing what the team identified as next steps:

> I think we all agree that one area we need to focus on is the use of formative assessment to adjust instruction in real time. During our observations, we've all noted instances where students were struggling with a concept, but the lesson continued as planned. What I heard you say is that when you meet again, you've agreed to explore some strategies for quickly gathering and responding to formative evidence during lessons. Is that correct? Overall, what you're doing is excellent work, and I'm excited to see how you continue to grow together. Please let me know what support you

> need from me moving forward. I'm committed to providing the resources and coaching necessary for you to keep refining your practice and achieving strong outcomes for our students.

Throughout the meeting, the principal used her influence to coach and guide her team. She drew on input and feedback from the team.

Tapping Into the Sources of Efficacy

Through coaching feedback, principals can persuade teachers to adopt new strategies, modify their current practices, or change their approach to teaching. By creating a supportive and collaborative environment, principals are more likely to persuade teachers to be open to feedback and willing to implement changes.

As a result, the feedback the principal gave had a totally different effect. Disentangling the coaching feedback from the evaluative feedback motivated the team for a renewed approach. After a few minor adjustments, the school team continued to gain momentum. Furthermore, they were able to adopt some of the coaching strategies into their practice to become even more precise and focused. Normalizing coaching feedback to focus on the process rather than the performance can strengthen collective efficacy.

Emphasizing the Role of Effort and Strategy Use

When providing feedback, by emphasizing the role of effort and strategy use, school principals focus on the processes and actions that teachers and teams take in achieving their goals. This is the essence of Carol Dweck's (2006, 2017) concept of a growth mindset applied to teachers as continuous learners. Leaders can help reduce the effects of the attribution bias when they are intentional in providing attributional feedback. *Attributional feedback* makes the cause-and-effect relationship more explicit by linking performance outcomes with effort, effective use of strategies, and skills and ability. Research indicates a positive correlation between attributional feedback and self-beliefs and academic achievement (Martinez & Huber, 2019; Schunk, 2003). Just like teachers would do with the students in their classrooms, school principals can help instill a growth mindset in teachers by discussing specific strategies and efforts and offering concrete suggestions on how to improve.

Tapping Into the Sources of Efficacy

School leaders can employ persuasive techniques to illuminate the causal connections between teaching and learning. Through feedback, principals can help teachers realize the cause-and-effect relationships that occur in schools.

By understanding the role of attributional feedback, principals can help teachers develop efficacy beliefs that facilitate motivation and performance. This type of persuasion helps educators realize mastery moments through language that focuses on a growth mindset. Table 1.1 illustrates examples of attributional feedback.

Readers might recall Carol Dweck's (1975, 2006, 2017) famous studies on fixed and growth mindsets, which demonstrate that teaching students to attribute failure to low effort or insufficient strategy use enhances students' expectations for success. Dweck also indicates that praising students for their intelligence can have detrimental effects.

Table 1.1: Examples of Attributional Feedback

Type of Attributional Feedback	Sounds Like . . .
Effort	"You really went that extra mile. The efforts of the team really paid off. Look at the progress the students made because of all your hard work."
Strategy Use	"Did you notice how well that strategy worked? The insights the students shared were very advanced and the comparisons they made were relevant and meaningful. The way you introduced and used the columns in the comparison matrix was very well scaffolded. That strategy was very effective for this particular learning outcome."
Skills and Ability	"It's obvious that you possess a very comprehensive knowledge of your subject area. Your ability to organize facts and information and present them in ways the students can grasp is impressive." (Note that feedback on skills and abilities, when framed correctly, can actually support a growth mindset rather than a fixed one. The key is to focus on the development and application of skills and abilities, rather than treating them as innate or unchangeable traits. When providing feedback on skills and abilities, school leaders should emphasize the process of skill development, the potential for improvement, and the connection between effort and growth in these areas.)

When providing feedback, it's important to determine whether teachers are in the early stages of learning a new strategy. If the teacher is a novice user of the strategy, they would benefit from effort-based feedback. This might sound like the following.

> It was obvious that you put a lot of effort into planning the jigsaw. There are many aspects to the jigsaw strategy that make it effective, and in this lesson, I observed students using social and conversational skills very effectively. I know you have been putting a lot of effort into improving classroom discussion and it shows.

In a meta-analysis examining the relationship between efficacy and performance, researchers Dana H. Lindsley, Daniel J. Brass, and James B. Thomas (1995) note that for teams to make self-correcting adjustments, "simple success/failure information is not sufficient" (p. 653). Teams need "accurate, timely, specific feedback regarding an understanding of cause-and-effect relationships involved in performing the task" (Lindsley et al., 1995, p. 653).

Educational psychologist Dale H. Schunk (2003) finds it is advantageous to provide effort feedback in the early stages of learning, but attributions should change as skills develop. Linking success to effective use of strategies and skills is more desirable for motivation in later stages of learning. This might sound like the following.

- "Your classroom management skills helped create a positive learning environment and foster a sense of community among your students."
- "You adapted and provided scaffolding to your multilingual students in the moment. That is a skill many teachers take a long time to develop. Did you notice how that scaffolding provided your students the additional support they needed?"

When providing feedback, by emphasizing the role of effort and strategy use, principals can help teachers engage in deeper reflection in light of evidence.

As noted in the introduction (page 1), efficacy increases when teachers make a direct link between their efforts and resulting positive outcomes. By increasing the use of cause-and-effect language, principals use persuasion to help teachers interpret their success through a growth mindset and thus shed light on mastery moments.

Providing Frequent Updating

Updating is about regularly sharing information, progress, and successes with the faculty to reinforce a sense of collective efficacy. Urban studies scholars Reinout Kleinhan and Gideon Bolt's (2013) research highlights that perceptions of efficacy are malleable, arising from a process that includes updating. Learning involves revising our thinking based on new information. In the absence of new information—that is, frequent feedback regarding evidence of impact—efficacy is unlikely to change. Therefore, feedback updating teachers about circumstances and results is necessary to realize mastery and therefore, foster a greater sense of efficacy in schools. It's too late to wait for the results of standardized tests. School principals can look for regular opportunities to provide teachers with updated information about students' progress and achievement. Updating helps create a sense of momentum and reinforces the belief that educators within the school are capable of overcoming challenges.

A classic example of how updating helped foster a greater sense of efficacy is the response to the 2011 tsunami that hit Fukushima, Japan, and devastated two nuclear power plants. One of the plants, Daini, was back under control within a few days while the other, Daiichi, was unable to prevent the meltdown of all four of its nuclear reactors (Gulati, Casto, & Krontiris, 2014). Collective efficacy's effectiveness explains why the team at Daini had better communication and how updating helped them regain control.

According to Hattie's (2023) Visible Learning synthesis, scaffolding has an effect size of 0.52.

Just like the workers at Daiichi, the workers at Daini were reeling from the natural disaster's devastation and trying to cope with the uncertainty of what was next. Their efficacy was just as much at risk. Rather than simply making decisions and issuing orders, the managers at Daini knew they had to use persuasion to rally their workers. The managers mitigated uncertainty and doubt and arrived at a common understanding with the team by providing continuous updates. They revised and communicated what they knew so that together they could adapt and respond accordingly. As a result, scholars Ranjay Gulati, Charles Casto, and Charlotte Krontiris (2014) explain, they didn't lose focus at the Daini plant.

Gulati and colleagues (2014) wrote a detailed account of the events at the Daini power plant for *Harvard Business Review*. They indicate that when the task of cooling down three of the four reactors was in jeopardy, Daini managers needed to persuade the team to venture out to examine the damage up close. They had to balance the need for immediacy and the delicate art of persuasion. The managers used a whiteboard to depict the frequency and magnitude of the aftershocks—trying to convince the workers that the danger of venturing out was decreasing.

Gulati and colleagues (2014) note that the management team gave the workers an opportunity to confront and process the uncertainty for themselves and encouraged them to reflect on how their evolving understanding fit their assessment of risk. After the managers presented the data, all workers agreed to survey the damage. When the reports came in, workers created a list of operational priorities. While workers made plans, managers shared information throughout the plant as it became available. This regular updating slowly replaced *uncertainty* with *meaning*. On the morning of March 15, 2011, as the Daiichi plant was scrambling to deal with its third explosion, all four Daini reactors achieved a cold shutdown.

The management team at Daini recognized the power of persuasion as an efficacy-enhancing source. Not only did the management team at Daini use persuasion to strengthen efficacy, but they also helped to reduce ambiguity and uncertainty that would weaken the workers' sense of efficacy. By sharing information as it became available, managers helped workers make sense of the situation.

Tapping Into the Sources of Efficacy

When principals ensure that teachers have up-to-date information about student progress, they are using the art of persuasion to help teachers to see the effect of their joint efforts on student outcomes.

The staff at Jennie P. Stewart Elementary School in Centerville, Utah, serve as a real-world example of how frequent updating helps foster a sense of efficacy in schools. T. J. Naylor, the principal at Stewart, was determined to create a culture of growth on arriving at the school. He was concerned that the population of students identified as needing special education was high, so he asked staff to focus on Tier 1 instruction.

The staff were learning new methods in phonics instruction. When meeting daily in grade-level bands, teams examined formative assessments that teachers were using regularly in their classrooms. They were looking for what the students could do and what they were struggling with, and reworking student groupings based on identified strengths and needs. Holding weekly student-assistance team meetings, Mr. Naylor presented data and teachers interpreted that data together. Most teachers brought data from one student that they were most concerned about. First- and second-grade teacher Claudia Janke reported that rather than worrying about just their own students in their own classrooms, teachers were able to address student learning needs together (USBE Teaching and Learning, 2023).

When teachers were updated about the positive changes in the students, they were inspired. Teachers observed students growing at rates they had not seen before. Updating at Jennie P. Stewart Elementary School was happening daily, meaning that teachers could adjust their instruction based on information about students' needs more frequently. Doing so helped them get better results. They realized they were achieving success through their combined efforts.

Collective Impact

Collective impact is the ultimate goal for school leaders striving to overcome the blame game and foster a culture of growth and learning. Educators working together can achieve remarkable results. By providing efficacy-enhancing feedback, principals can empower teachers to recognize the power of their collective efforts and the positive impact they can have on student outcomes. School leaders can create environments where feedback is normalized, effort and effective strategy use are celebrated, and frequent updates on progress are shared. By doing so, they will unleash the potential of teacher teams, inspire them to embrace challenges, and ultimately drive collective impact that will transform the lives of students. The power to overcome blame and achieve greatness lies within the school community—and leaders of efficacy can harness it through effective feedback.

Blame is an enemy of efficacy because when blame is placed on external sources, educators miss the impact they can make by collaborating and using effective strategies. An effective efficacy builder can overcome the blame game and help teachers realize success through effective feedback. Micro-moves in this chapter include normalizing coaching feedback, emphasizing the role of effort and strategy use, and providing frequent updating. Use the exercises and prompts in the reproducible "Planning for Action to Overcome Blame" (page 24) to practice delivering feedback in a way that will enhance teacher efficacy.

Planning for Action to Overcome Blame

Use the following prompts to reflect on how you might implement the micro-moves discussed in chapter 1.

Normalizing Coaching Feedback

How might you disentangle evaluative feedback from coaching feedback?

What opportunities can you identify to provide coaching feedback? Who will provide it and when will they provide it?

Emphasizing the Role of Effort and Strategy Use

Identify teachers or teams who would benefit from effort-based feedback. What are they working toward? What opportunities can you identify to provide feedback to these teachers or teams? What cause-effect language will you use?

Identify teachers or teams who would benefit from strategy-based feedback. What strategies are they currently using? What opportunities can you identify to provide feedback to these teachers or teams? What cause-effect language will you use?

Identify teachers or teams who would benefit from skills and ability feedback. What skills or abilities can you highlight? What opportunities can you identify to provide feedback to these teachers or teams? What cause-effect language will you use?

Providing Frequent Updating

What is your staff working to improve? What data can you access regularly that will help them see progress?

When and how will you share data to update teachers about their progress?

Chapter 2

Perspective Over Magnitude

By *framing challenges appropriately*, school leaders can overcome *magnitude* as an enemy of efficacy.

In this chapter, we explore how magnitude functions as an enemy of efficacy. When teachers view problems or tasks as too big or too complex, it has a negative impact on their efficacy. By using the framing effect, school leaders can overcome magnitude. Three key micro-moves leaders can employ include framing through emphasizing and de-emphasizing, framing different futures, and framing challenges into smaller pieces. School leaders achieve collective impact as they overcome magnitude by framing challenges appropriately.

Magnitude as an Enemy of Efficacy

Magnitude comes into play when individuals and teams form efficacy beliefs (Bandura, 1977). If teachers perceive that the magnitude of the challenge is too big, then efficacy becomes fragile. We introduced the four sources of efficacy earlier (page 2). These include mastery experiences, vicarious experiences, persuasion, and feelings or emotions. Bandura (1982) notes that although these sources influence efficacy beliefs, it is the cognitive appraisal of these experiences that ultimately determine efficacy. As individuals and teams process efficacy sources, they also analyze the requirements of the task (Goddard et al., 2000). Figure 2.1 (page 28) outlines this process. If an individual or team perceives that the magnitude of the challenge is too big or the task is too difficult, efficacy is at risk.

Doubt creeps in. Teams may start to question whether they have the ability or resources they need to tackle the challenge. As doubts grow, motivation to put in the necessary effort decreases. When educators believe that their efforts won't amount to much, they give up more easily and lack the resolve they need to improve the

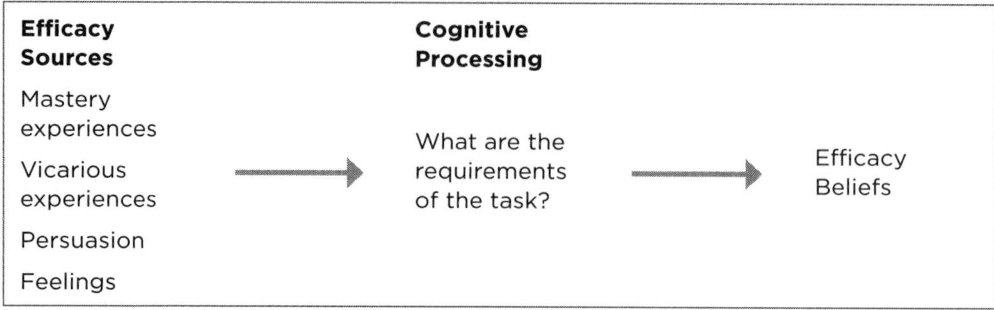

Figure 2.1. Forming efficacy beliefs.

situation. This is a negative self-fulfilling prophecy at work. When teams believe they can't reach a goal, they unconsciously behave in ways that make that belief a reality. They may put forth less effort, take fewer risks, or make more mistakes, ultimately undermining their own success. The efficacy-performance relationship is a cyclical one. That is, bad performance weakens efficacy, which in turn further affects performance, and so on.

In addition, when team members lose confidence in their collective ability, they may be less likely to collaborate effectively. Communication, coordination, and mutual support may suffer as individuals focus on their own concerns and doubts. Furthermore, setbacks are magnified. When team members perceive a task as too challenging, any setbacks or obstacles they encounter along the way can seem insurmountable. Teams may be more likely to become discouraged and give up when faced with difficulties rather than persisting and problem solving. Consider the following example.

A high school, labeled as "failing" based on performance scores, was listed in the bottom 5 percent of all schools in the state for the third year in a row. Not having shown much growth, and with just a minimal improvement in the graduation rate, the school was under intensive review. Teachers and school leaders were faced with additional accountability and increased pressure to demonstrate improved student outcomes. The real dilemma, however, was that the collective efficacy the school needed to organize and execute the courses of action to demonstrate improvement was lacking. Over the course of the previous five years, with the declining academic status of the school, teacher turnover was extensive. Educators lowered their expectations and began to doubt their capacity to improve the performance of low-achieving students. A weakened sense of collective efficacy resulted in reluctance to take risks, reduced efforts, and a lack of commitment to school-improvement goals.

The correlation between lack of effort and commitment and lower performance at the school was significant. Furthermore, the teachers and school leaders perceived the challenge of moving out of their state's bottom-performing 5 percent of schools as too great, given the school's demographics and current trajectory. Educators' perception of the magnitude of the challenge further reduced their efficacy and the school continued on a downward spiral.

To realize systemic and sustainable improvement in schools, principals can manage educators' perceptions of magnitude and strengthen collective efficacy. By understanding how perceptions of task difficulty can threaten collective efficacy, leaders can take proactive steps to support teams and maintain their shared belief in their ability to succeed. Leaders can persuasively use framing techniques so that teachers do not feel overwhelmed by the magnitude of challenges they face. It's in these environments where a sense of perspective leads to learning and growth. School leaders can take intentional steps to overcome magnitude as an enemy of efficacy.

Researchers Wayne K. Hoy, Scott R. Sweetland, and Page A. Smith (2002) state, "leadership that is calm in the face of conflict goes a long way toward limiting misinterpretation of events and either over- or underreaction" (p. 91).

Overcome Magnitude With Framing

School principals can overcome magnitude and strengthen collective efficacy through framing effects. *Framing* is a persuasive technique principals can use to influence how teachers perceive and respond to information. Understanding the effects of framing is the first step. Next, by using a few simple framing techniques, principals can influence how teachers think about challenges and ultimately impact how teachers approach their work. Principals can use framing techniques to minimize how teachers perceive the magnitude of the challenges within their school community.

Framing is an angle of view—a way in which school leaders look at things. A frame is how leaders see a situation and approach an issue. In the social sciences, framing is a set of concepts influencing how individuals, groups, and societies organize, perceive, and communicate about reality (Reese, Gandy, & Grant, 2001). Principals often frame how they see challenges without being aware of it.

Framing is often used in business, media, and politics as a persuasive technique to influence attitudes and behaviors. The simple definition of the framing effect is that people respond differently to the same objective fact because of different descriptions. Framing effects have been studied in many domains. Studies show that public opinion over wrongful convictions are contingent on how information is framed (Norris & Mullinix, 2020). In another study, framing influenced donor responses to nonprofit charities (Qu & Daniel, 2020). The effects of framing were also studied in relation to the public's responses to the COVID-19 pandemic.

In the previous section's example, the focus, or frame, was a deficit mindset. The frame about being in the bottom 5 percent of all schools in the state dominated the focus and weakened educators' efficacy. Principals can help teachers conceptualize a different frame by calling attention to certain points of focus. If we consider a frame as a metaphor, it is like placing an imaginary frame around a situation—calling into focus a certain view or perspective. Place a gold frame around a painting, it will bring out the gold in the work. Place a red frame around the same work, and the red in the painting will be more pronounced. Three framing techniques that serve as micromoves include (1) emphasizing and de-emphasizing certain aspects of the situation, (2) framing different futures, and (3) framing the challenge into smaller pieces.

Framing Through Emphasizing and De-Emphasizing

Principals can garner support from teachers and help them to think differently about challenges by emphasizing certain messages and de-emphasizing others. Start by figuring out the answers to the following questions.

- What positive information can I emphasize?
- What information do I need to de-emphasize?

Returning to the earlier high school example, when a new school leader came into the school, she felt stuck with the answer to the first question since the school did not yet have a lot of progress or growth to highlight. So instead of addressing the first question, the new principal began to find opportunities to highlight the things teachers were doing that positively impacted student achievement. While there were a lot of challenges at the school, the new principal knew that she could find small but powerful messages to amplify. Consider the following examples.

- A team of teachers selected a few students at risk and used the 2 × 10 strategy. The 2 × 10 strategy is about consistently building relationships with students. Teachers set a goal to engage in a two-minute conversation with the selected students for ten consecutive school days. What did they notice? These students started to attend classes more regularly, they smiled more often, and teachers learned more about their students' likes and dislikes.

- Teachers in the mathematics department were focused on increasing student discussion in their classrooms. The teachers were using a strategy called successive pair share to help students revise their own work. After teachers provided an equation for students to solve independently, students shared the steps they used to reach a solution with a partner. After hearing what worked from their classmate, each student had an opportunity to revise their work and then continue the process with a new partner. Most students welcomed the opportunity to get out of their seats and talk with their classmates and over time, teachers noticed improvements in student work.

According to Hattie's (2023) Visible Learning synthesis, teacher-student relationships have an effect size of 0.48.

While these two research-based strategies (teacher-student relationships and classroom discussion) did not yet yield positive results on the state test, by highlighting them, the new school principal was demonstrating what she valued and by doing so, encouraged more of it. The strategies were not overwhelming or difficult to implement, and some teachers were willing to try them because they saw how they worked for their colleagues.

Tapping Into the Sources of Efficacy

The vicarious experiences of witnessing their colleagues succeed with specific strategies helped other teachers in the high school develop a willingness to try new strategies. When teachers see other teachers in their school meet with even a small success, it helps in building their efficacy vicariously.

According to Hattie's (2023) Visible Learning synthesis, classroom discussion has an effect size of 0.82.

While teachers were reluctant to share at first, it became more of the norm over time. The school leaders ensured that the teachers shared the positive outcomes (for example, students smiling more often, improvements in their work) so that their colleagues' focus was on something manageable they could do to make a positive difference. By emphasizing the small steps a few teachers in the building were taking, the new principal was beginning to reframe the challenge and focus teachers' attention on the positive things they could observe in their school.

Tapping Into the Sources of Efficacy

The high school example demonstrates how teachers are influenced through social persuasion. Teachers' beliefs about their own abilities and potential for success are influenced by other teachers.

When using framing techniques to help teachers perceive challenges as more manageable, a leader might emphasize the following.

- **Available resources and support:** Highlight the resources, professional learning, and support systems in place to assist teachers in tackling the challenge.
- **Past successes:** Remind teachers of similar challenges they have successfully overcome in the past, boosting their confidence and efficacy.
- **Collective effort:** Emphasize that the team will address challenges together, with collaboration and shared responsibility among staff members.
- **Growth opportunities:** Frame the challenge as an opportunity for professional growth, skill development, and innovation.
- **Positive outcomes:** Focus on the potential positive outcomes for students, teachers, and the community once teachers successfully address the challenge.
- **Resilience and adaptability:** Highlight the resilience and adaptability of the teaching staff, emphasizing their capacity to overcome obstacles.
- **Alignment with school values:** Connect the challenge to the school's core values, mission, and vision, giving staff a sense of purpose and importance.

Emphasizing becomes important when helping staff to understand the relationship between the school's vision and district and state policy initiatives and priorities. By strategically emphasizing these aspects, a principal can help teachers view challenges as more manageable and approachable, fostering a positive and proactive mindset.

De-emphasizing certain messages is just as important as emphasizing others while reframing challenges in schools. Leaders can de-emphasize the following aspects of a challenge: complexity, uncertainty, and time pressure.

- To de-emphasize complexity, school leaders can simplify a challenge to make it seem more manageable.
- When de-emphasizing uncertainty, principals can highlight what is known and certain. This provides a stable foundation for decision making and action; it can also help reduce the anxiety and paralysis that often come with too much focus on unknowns.
- Excessive focus on time constraints can lead to stress and rushed decisions, so it's important for principals to de-emphasize time pressure. While deadlines are often important, leaders can instead emphasize steady progress and quality work.

In addition to de-emphasizing these aspects of a challenge, leaders can also build staff efficacy by minimizing discussions about factors beyond the school's control. Minimizing such discussions will help to focus the faculty's energy on areas where they can actually make a difference. It also empowers teachers by emphasizing their agency and ability to effect change. By taking this approach, leaders can create a more positive and productive environment for addressing challenges. De-emphasizing doesn't mean ignoring real complexities, uncertainties, or time constraints, but rather framing the challenge in a way that feels more approachable and actionable.

A principal can help create a more positive and empowering narrative around challenges, encouraging teachers to focus on the actionable steps and available support systems rather than getting bogged down by potential obstacles or negative thoughts.

Framing Different Futures

When considering what *could be*, Hedley Beare's (2001) framework for thinking about the future can be very useful for educators (Earl & Katz, 2006). Beare (2001) identifies three kinds of futures.

1. **Possible futures:** Futures that could happen, some of which are likely; most are unlikely to be.
2. **Probable futures:** Futures that will happen unless something intervenes to throw them off course.
3. **Preferable futures:** Futures that you prefer to happen and that you will plan to make happen.

Each student has a probable future—a path they may follow based on their current circumstances and societal expectations. However, educators can disrupt these probable futures and help students design preferable futures that align with their aspirations and potential. Framing different futures is about helping teachers envision preferable futures and understand their role in making them happen.

Consider the following ways school leaders can frame the concept of designing preferable futures for students and disrupting probable futures.

- Discuss educators' opportunities to shape their students' lives.
- Describe both probable and preferable futures (for example, preferable futures are those in which students are able to break free from the limitations placed on them by society, economic status, or personal challenges).
- Use high-expectations language (believing in the potential of every student and challenging the notion of predetermined outcomes).
- Challenge teachers to reflect on their role in shaping students' futures and how they can design learning experiences that not only impart knowledge but also inspire students to become agents of change in their own lives.

Bandura (1998) notes that people's beliefs in their efficacy "influence the anticipatory scenarios and visualized futures they construct and rehearse. Those of high efficacy visualize success scenarios that provide guides for performance. Those who doubt their efficacy visualize failure scenarios that undermine performance" (p. 58).

To frame a different future is to envision it and describe what it would look like in the very best-case scenario. Principals can initiate discussions into the steps, players, actions, and timelines needed to be successful. Together, educators can intentionally design preferable futures for their students and disrupt probable futures.

Tapping Into the Sources of Efficacy

By framing different futures, principals use persuasive language designed to inspire and motivate educators, such as "disrupt these probable futures," "design preferable futures," and "be agents of change." This language can persuade educators to view their role as transformative and believe in their ability to make a significant impact on students' lives.

Framing Challenges Into Smaller Pieces

Another framing technique principals can use when teachers feel overwhelmed by the magnitude of the challenge is to break it down into manageable pieces. Look at the big picture and then think small. Break down complex issues into specific, actionable steps. Instead of presenting a challenge as a monolithic problem, principals can work with teachers to identify the key components of the issue and develop a step-by-step plan to address each aspect. This approach makes the challenge feel more manageable and provides a clear road map for progress.

Principals can help teachers prioritize the most pressing aspects of the challenge, ensuring they direct resources and efforts toward the areas that will have the greatest impact. By focusing on a few key priorities at a time, teachers can avoid feeling overwhelmed by the entirety of the challenge. It is also helpful for principals to schedule regular check-ins with teachers to review progress, discuss any new challenges that have arisen, and reassess priorities as needed. By maintaining open lines of communication and being flexible in the face of changing circumstances, principals can help teachers stay focused on the most critical issues while also being responsive to emerging needs.

Marketing scholar Jonah Berger (2020) uses the phrase "chunking the change" (p. 113) and suggests that by breaking big asks into smaller, more manageable chunks and adding "stepping stones along the way" (p. 114) people will be much more willing to take the journey. Finally, as teachers accomplish each step, it is important to acknowledge the small wins. Journalist and author Charles Duhigg (2014) notes that "once a small win has been accomplished, forces are set in motion that favor another small win. Small wins fuel transformative changes by leveraging tiny advantages into patterns that convince people that bigger achievements are within reach" (p. 112).

Tapping Into the Sources of Efficacy

By presenting ideas in a clear and supportive manner, principals can persuade teachers to embrace the process of breaking down challenges into smaller pieces, ultimately leading to more effective problem solving and a more positive work environment.

Collective Impact

When school leaders effectively use framing techniques to manage educators' perceptions of the magnitude of challenges, they unlock the power of collective efficacy to drive transformative change. By emphasizing positive aspects, envisioning preferable futures, and breaking down challenges into manageable steps, principals can inspire their teams to approach even the most daunting tasks with optimism, determination, and a shared belief in their collective ability to succeed. School leaders have the power to shape the narrative and help teachers see challenges as opportunities for growth and achievement. By consistently applying these framing techniques, efficacy builders will create a culture of resilience, where staff meet obstacles with creativity, collaboration, and unwavering commitment to student success. Realizing collective impact begins with a shift in perspective and school leaders can guide teams toward a vision of what's possible.

Negative affective states reduce efficacy (Bandura, 1998). When teachers feel stressed and anxious, it places their efficacy at risk.

Magnitude is an enemy of efficacy because when teachers perceive the magnitude of the challenge as too large, their efficacy is at risk. An effective efficacy builder can reduce teachers' perceptions of the magnitude of the challenge through framing effects. Framing effects present information in ways that change or influence the behavior of others. Three micro-move framing techniques we outlined in this chapter include framing through emphasizing and de-emphasizing, framing different futures, and framing challenges into smaller pieces. It's advantageous for school principals to be ready to frame communications both prepared and spontaneously. Use the exercises and prompts in the reproducible "Planning for Action to Overcome Magnitude" (page 37) to practice framing techniques so that you can better communicate with teachers to address the impact of magnitude.

Planning for Action to Overcome Magnitude

Use the following exercises and prompts to engage with the micro-moves discussed in chapter 2.

Framing Through Emphasizing and De-Emphasizing

Identify three positive messages to emphasize.

Who will share these messages? How and when will they share them?

Identify what to de-emphasize.

Who will share these messages? How and when with they share them?

Framing Different Futures

Effective efficacy builders can help teachers visualize preferable futures using a modified version of a futures protocol (National School Reform Faculty, n.d.). Use the following steps as a guide.

Step 1: Look Forward

Talk in present tense. Share what you are trying to accomplish and what it will look like when it is done. Project into the future (whatever timeline seems appropriate) and describe the best-case scenario. Do not describe *how*; instead, focus on what it would feel like, sound like, and look like accomplishing the goal (for example, five years later in a school's reform efforts). Use storytelling to imagine the best-case scenario and focus on opportunities rather than obstacles. It's helpful to chart this information so that the group can refer back to what has been said.

Step 2: Look Back

Talk in past tense. Look back from the projected future and describe how what the team was trying to accomplish looked when they started. Think about issues, culture, conversations, teachers' work, and student achievement. Try to remain as tangible as possible. It's helpful to continue to chart information and record dates to identify the time periods you are referring to.

Step 3: Continue to Look Back

Continue to talk in the past tense. Continue to look back from the projected future. Discuss how the team got started and how you moved from that to the projected future. Directly relate the previous description of how what the team was trying to accomplish looked when they started. Consider discussing how, when, with what resources, and by whom the goal was accomplished.

Framing Challenges Into Smaller Pieces

What do teachers perceive as their biggest challenge?

What are some specific steps you can identify to help break the challenge into more manageable pieces?

How and when will you share the steps with teachers?

Reference

National School Reform Faculty. (n.d.). NSRF protocols and activities . . . From A to Z. *Accessed at https://nsrfharmony.org/protocols on June 26, 2024.*

Chapter 3

Commitment Over Compliance

By *garnering commitment*, school leaders can overcome *compliance* as an enemy of efficacy.

In this chapter, we notice how compliance acts as an enemy of efficacy. School leaders can overcome compliance by creating cultures of commitment. Three key micro-moves leaders can use include highlighting a gap, learning from marker students, and surfacing the cost of inaction. School leaders achieve collective impact as they overcome compliance through garnering commitment.

Compliance as an Enemy of Efficacy

Imagine a spectrum with compliance at one end and commitment at the other. At the compliance end, power and control rest with a select few individuals who determine how things should work. Principals use their authority to ensure that teachers do the things they're meant to be doing when they're meant to be done. As a result, policies get superficially implemented and teachers don't necessarily feel that their voices and opinions matter. Therefore, compliance can be an enemy of efficacy.

At the commitment end of the spectrum, power and decision making are distributed more broadly, with teachers actively involved in shaping policies and practices. In this environment, educators feel a strong sense of ownership and investment in their work, leading to more authentic implementation of initiatives and a greater sense of collective efficacy.

Figure 3.1 (page 42) illustrates this dynamic.

Researchers Christopher J. F. Burke and Martha Adler (2013) demonstrate how compliance can be an enemy of efficacy in their case study of two fifth-grade

Figure 3.1: Commitment over compliance spectrum.

teachers dealing with district mandates. In the years prior to the study, the researchers discovered that the district had a history of low academic achievement and reform efforts had become increasingly driven by state and federal mandates. Burke and Adler (2013) write, "The perpetual reform cycle results in constant changing of teachers' roles without any evidence of significant changes in student achievement; the top-down mandates challenged teacher autonomy and instituted prescriptive solutions" (p. 7). They describe how teachers complied with a required pacing guide for reading and writing even though they felt it limited their abilities to respond to students' needs.

The newly introduced common assessments and pacing guide required that all students read the same text during the same two-week time frame. Teachers complied in the first year even though they felt the books were "inappropriate for their students' reading levels and lacked cultural relevance" (Burke & Adler, 2013, p. 11). One of the teachers described her compliance with the pacing guide in that first year as "plodding through in a superficial manner" (Burke & Adler, 2013, p. 11) while expressing concern that the curriculum required them to teach to the test, resulting in lost opportunities for discussion and extension activities. Teacher efficacy was at risk.

Over time, the teachers increasingly engaged in what Burke and Adler (2013) described as "small acts of defiance" (p. 14) while deviating from the pacing guide. Instead, they planned lessons "framed by their understandings of culturally relevant pedagogy, and effective instruction, and informed by their insights into the students' academic needs" (Burke & Adler, 2013, p. 13). The researchers described a shift from compliance to "acts of resistance" (p. 12) and teachers began "teaching behind closed doors, not sharing at grade-level meetings what they were teaching and making their 'official' lesson plans less and less specific" (p. 14).

To be clear, we're not suggesting that teachers should be exempt from complying with key policies. It's imperative that schools adhere to legislation and policy frameworks. Tightly following student protection policies and ensuring financial and safety audits are completed are a must. In these instances, compliance is critical. When referring to compliance, our intention is to capture the mindset of the leaders. Are principals open to learning and growing the team? Or are leaders set on how things are going to be done and determined to enforce their way?

In the previous example, because the district struggled to make annual yearly progress, the administration responded by centralizing the curriculum and instructional decision-making process, believing this to be "the best way to directly align instruction with the state assessment" (Burke & Adler, 2013, p. 14). Burke and Adler further state that "sadly, both teachers' efforts to adapt the curriculum to be engaging, culturally relevant, integrated and focus on students' needs were devalued by administrators" (p. 14). The result: teachers reacted to "district initiatives in resistant ways, while 'acting' in compliance" (p. 14).

To realize systemic and sustainable improvements in schools, principals can create cultures of commitment. Leaders can use persuasion to move away from the compliance end of the spectrum toward commitment, therefore realizing better outcomes and enhancing collective teacher efficacy. It's in these environments where sticking to priorities leads to learning and growth. System and school leaders can take intentional steps to overcome compliance as an enemy of efficacy.

Overcome Compliance With Commitment

Principals can garner commitment to overcome compliance and strengthen collective efficacy. Surprisingly, when principals have achieved a strong sense of commitment with their faculty, compliance indicators actually *improve* as team members realize the importance that their role has in helping others and ensuring the non-negotiables are embedded throughout the school. Principals can spark a sense of purpose to increase commitment and influence a range of productive behaviors in the school.

Teaching and leading in schools are too difficult to accomplish independently. Collective commitment is needed and schools must embrace the challenge to harness the power of the collective. Garnering commitment starts, however, with principals demonstrating their devotion to the mission and vision of the school and leading with the courage to engage in difficult but necessary conversations. Next, school leaders can overcome a compliance mindset and build a strong sense of commitment by sparking a sense of purpose.

The reason that most teachers enter the field of education is because of their desire to make a difference for children. When we talk to teachers about why they stay in the profession, their reasons are often because they want to instill a love for learning in their students and provide them with opportunities to grow and succeed. They want to see their students make progress and live up to their full potential. They want what is best for students. This is their sense of purpose. By reigniting educators' sense of purpose, leaders can garner the commitment needed to realize improved results.

The three micro-moves for doing so include (1) highlighting a gap, (2) learning from marker students, and (3) surfacing the cost of inaction.

Highlighting a Gap

One way principals can spark a sense of purpose is to highlight a gap by presenting data in compelling ways. When used correctly, data can be helpful in providing actionable insights into student achievement. Data help educators measure student progress, evaluate program and instructional effectiveness, and, most importantly, ensure that every student learns. As teachers and teams realize progress, their efficacy is enhanced. However, it's important for principals to decipher what data are most meaningful and avoid using data in haphazard ways. Andrea Evans (2009) states that "leaders determine what information gets used or omitted, whether the information is accurate, who gets the information, and how the information is to be used" (p. 83).

Teachers want to make a difference for all their students; that is their purpose. Unfortunately, not all students' current pathway is leading them to success, and which students fail is too often predicted by their family income, race, gender, and first language (Pizarro Milian et al., 2024). When leaders bring this to light by highlighting the gap, they spark a sense of purpose and increase teachers' commitment to making a difference for *all* their students.

Tapping Into the Sources of Efficacy

Highlighting a gap is a form of social persuasion because the aim is to influence educators' beliefs and motivate them to take action to address the disparities.

We witnessed this in a school district in San Jose, California. Teacher teams engaged in cycles of inquiry to identify student learning needs and determine strategies for addressing those needs. During the first meeting, the organizers shared data (see figure 3.2, page 45) that demonstrated the difference in mathematics proficiency between non-Latinx students and Latinx students in the elementary, middle, and high schools in the district.

As teachers made sense of the data, they uncovered a big gap—that the Latinx students were significantly underperforming in mathematics as compared to non-Latinx students beginning in elementary school and continuing into high school. Most teachers in the room were surprised and upset at the realization. They hadn't seen the data presented this way in the past. They had only examined overall achievement scores.

By presenting the disaggregated data and highlighting a gap, the organizers helped to create a discrepancy between how things currently were and how they would like things to be. By sharing the gap in mathematics achievement between non-Latinx and

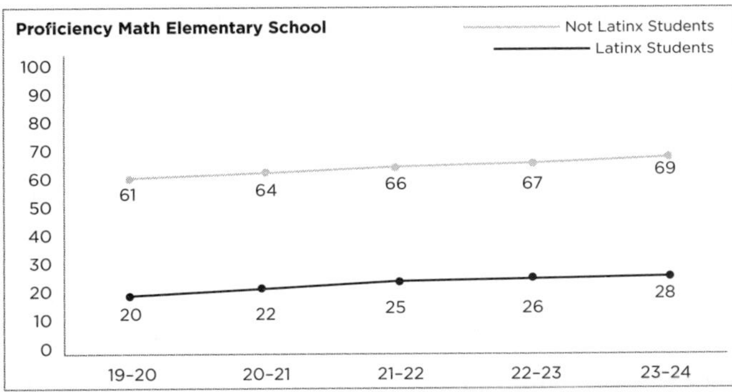

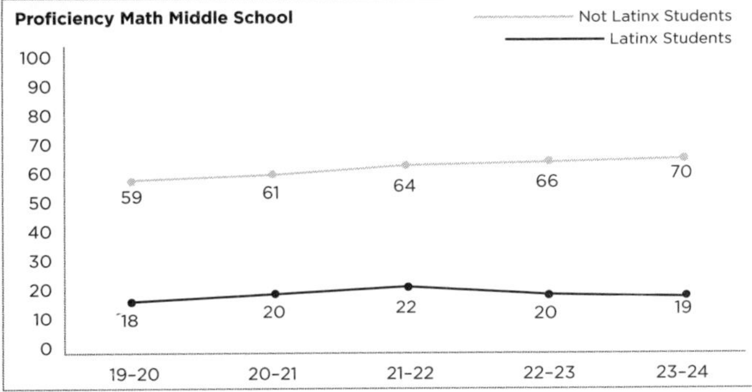

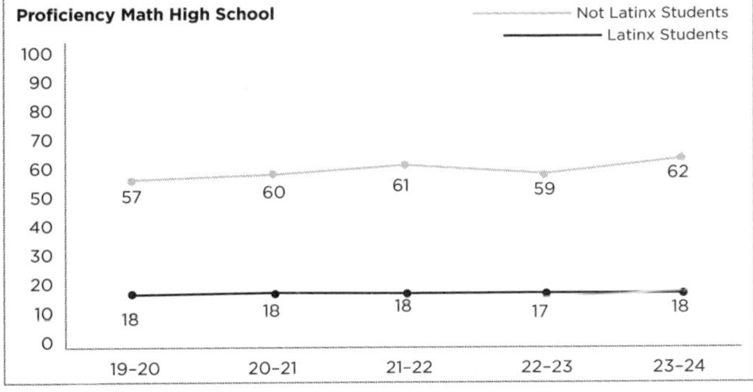

Figure 3.2: Mathematics proficiency for non-Latinx versus Latinx students.

In examining the impact of leadership on student outcomes, researchers Viviane M. J. Robinson, Claire A. Lloyd, and Kenneth J. Rowe (2008) note that goal setting had an impact of 0.42. They also highlight that part of the process for activating goal-relevant behavior includes creating a discrepancy between current realities and desired future states.

Latinx students, leaders created a demand for the gap to be reduced and garnered greater commitment to achieving more equitable outcomes from the participating teachers. Upon seeing the disaggregated data, educators developed troubling discrepancies, realizing that maintaining the status quo wasn't really an option. Teachers were confronted with their own values in a way that helped create urgency and commitment to trying new strategies. As Berger (2020) writes, "people strive for internal consistency. They want their attitudes, beliefs, and behaviors to align" (p. 41).

Roger Goddard, Linda Skrla, and Serena J. Salloum (2017) examine the role of collective efficacy in closing the achievement gap. They find that the stronger a school's sense of collective efficacy, the higher the overall levels of mathematics achievement *and* the lower the disadvantage for Black students. One standard deviation increase in collective efficacy was associated with a 50 percent reduction in the academic disadvantage experienced by Black students. In addition, Latinx students did not score significantly differently than White students after accounting for their prior achievement, ethnicity, gender, and status with regard to English as an additional language, special education, and free or reduced-price lunch programs.

Through shared activities like examining disaggregated evidence, teachers receive "the opportunity to view problems as collective and view their colleagues as resources," according to educational policy scholar Serena J. Salloum (2021). She adds, "These interactions shape broad teacher attitudes and dispositions, as well as set norms such as teachers taking responsibility for student learning" (p. 239). This is a critical point for building efficacy. Suddenly, when colleagues are viewed as a collective resource, problems of practice seem less formidable. Highly efficacious teams capitalize on opportunities to meet for the purpose of learning from disaggregated student data and determining ways to decrease inequities.

Tapping Into the Sources of Efficacy

Highlighting a gap is a persuasive technique principals can use to motivate teachers by presenting data that reveal disparities in student achievement, particularly along lines of income, race, gender, and language. By strategically sharing this information, principals can tap into teachers' sense of purpose and reinforce their commitment to ensuring every student succeeds, regardless of background.

Learning From Marker Students

Another micro-move to help garner commitment and spark a sense of purpose is identifying marker students. A *marker student* is a "student of interest," as identified by a teacher. For example, the selected student might not be progressing as expected and the teacher is uncertain why. When implementing strategies, collaborating teachers help examine the marker student's progress over time and suggest next steps based on observations. As marker students improve, teachers' sense of purpose is reignited, and their efficacy is strengthened as they witness the positive effects of their own context-generated solutions. Individual marker students are often used as a "proxy for a wider group of students" (Donohoo & Katz, 2020, p. 78).

A vice principal led the first-grade team in learning from marker students. They focused on students requiring additional support, sharing their thinking while working through mathematics problems. Observing a marker student named Zac, one teacher noticed the student struggled to find the language to describe pattern attributes while using pattern blocks to create patterns. This led to teachers creating word walls in their classrooms. *Word walls* are collections of words displayed in a classroom that become an interactive tool for students to use during reading, writing, and problem solving. Zac's teacher used a whiteboard and added words as the unit on patterning progressed.

Over the next week, Zac's teacher noticed that he began to look to the word wall for the help he needed. As Zac worked with what he referred to as a "big and small" pattern, the teacher asked him to describe the attribute. Zac looked at the word wall and pointed to the word *size*. The teacher continued to make use of the word wall, and later in the unit Zac surprised them all. In a moment when he looked to the wall and the word he needed wasn't there, he walked up to the whiteboard with an erasable marker. He asked the vice principal, who was observing at the time, "How do you spell 'shrinking'?" When asked why he wrote the word *shrinking* on the whiteboard, Zac said, "So that others have it and it's there in case I need it later." Zac's co-construction of the word wall was very validating for the collaborating teachers. They also recognized that by closely monitoring a marker student, they received insights that allowed them to adjust their instruction to better meet students' needs. Not only Zac benefited—others did as well.

According to Hattie's (2023) Visible Learning synthesis, vocabulary strategies have an effect size of 0.62.

Tapping Into the Sources of Efficacy

Identifying marker students is a persuasive technique principals could use to convince teachers to adopt new strategies by showing them the tangible impact their efforts can have on individual students. By focusing on the progress of specific "students of interest," teachers can see the direct results of their context-generated solutions, boosting their sense of purpose and efficacy.

Principals can help teachers learn about and support marker students using the following steps.

1. **Identify marker students:** In every classroom, there are students not yet responding or ready to learn. Ask teachers to identify two to three marker students and write down what they know about their strengths, needs, and preferences. Teachers can also seek perspectives from their colleagues who know the students. Ask teachers to identify their wonderings about the marker students.
2. **Have marker students complete a task:** As students complete the task, teachers carefully analyze student thinking. This will help to identify strategies the student is currently using and areas of struggle that the team can use to inform next steps and identify instructional strategies.
3. **Support teachers as they implement strategies:** As teachers implement strategies, they document the impact on marker students. Encourage teachers to collaborate with colleagues regarding resources and instructional strategies to support marker students. Help teachers be attentive by noting how marker students respond to different types of instruction.
4. **Have marker students complete a second task:** This step helps teams gain information regarding impact and for determining next steps.

Surfacing the Cost of Inaction

The third micro-move for sparking a sense of purpose is to surface the cost of inaction by making educators aware of the *omission bias*. The omission bias happens when people prefer omission (inaction) over commission (action). People tend to judge harm as a result of commission more negatively than harm as a result of omission (Katz & Dack, 2013). Steven Katz and Lisa Ain Dack (2013) find that the omission bias impedes the kind of learning that results in permanent change in thinking and behavior. They explain that people "are so afraid of the potential downside of action that they sometimes choose inaction" (p. 63). However, people fail to grasp "that doing nothing is, in fact, doing something. There is no such thing as doing nothing. Nothing is what they are currently doing; it's a choice to preserve the status quo" (Katz & Dack, 2013, p. 63).

An example comes from our experience working with content area teachers in a high school. The district was investing professional development funds to help geography, science, history, mathematics, physical education, technology, and business teachers integrate literacy instruction into their daily practice. The teachers involved in the project agreed that many of their students were having difficulty comprehending the content in their courses. To try to meet students' needs, the district asked teachers to integrate metacognitive and literacy strategies such as anticipation guides and know-wonder-learn charts, and increase classroom discussion using think-pair-share and opinion lines.

Many of the teachers were hesitant to make the change because they were unsure of how they would maintain classroom management. They believed their students might misbehave or go off topic if given more freedom for discussion. The teachers felt that it was better to stay the course and continue to teach the way they always had—even though they recognized that comprehension was problematic for many of their students. As Katz and Dack (2013) point out, "doing nothing isn't really doing nothing—it's doing nothing *new*" (p. 63). Doing nothing new isn't risk neutral in this case, since the students in the content-area classes need reading and writing strategies to be more successful in those courses.

The principal, recognizing the teachers' hesitation, decided to address the omission bias head-on. She prepared for the next collaborative learning session and was ready to discuss the consequences of not implementing the new literacy strategies. She began by sharing students' current comprehension levels, highlighting the fact that many students were struggling. She projected the potential academic outcomes if no changes were made, including decreased graduation rates. And she also discussed how continuing with ineffective teaching methods could lead to increased frustration and burnout among teachers, as they would continually struggle to help students understand the material.

Initially, the teachers had mixed reactions. Many teachers were taken aback by the projected outcomes and expressed genuine concern for their students' futures. Some teachers initially became defensive, arguing that the projections were too pessimistic. A few teachers expressed feelings of guilt, realizing they might have been unknowingly hindering their students' progress. Teachers began asking questions about the new strategies, showing increased interest in learning more. And as the discussion progressed, more teachers started to acknowledge the need for change. The principal's approach of surfacing the cost of inaction helped shift the teachers' perspective from fearing the change to recognizing the need for action. By making the consequences of inaction tangible and personal, she was able to overcome the omission bias and spark a sense of purpose among the teaching staff.

Inaction isn't as costless as it seems. Berger (2020) notes it's more difficult to get people to change when things aren't terrible and that "average performance generates complacency" (p. 73). While the costs of change are mostly up front (for example, teachers need to invest time to learn a new program or curriculum), the benefits take longer to happen (for example, teachers don't see immediate improvements in student learning). Berger (2020) writes that "This cost-benefit timing gap stymies action" (p. 76). People are more likely to stick with the status quo rather than incur costs—especially when the status quo doesn't seem all that bad. Change leaders need to make it "easier for people to see the difference between what they are doing now and what they could be doing" (Berger, 2020, p. 77), and it's important to highlight how much people are *losing* by doing nothing.

Tapping Into the Sources of Efficacy

By surfacing the cost of inaction, principals use persuasion to make educators aware of the omission bias and the potential costs of not taking action. The strategy aims to motivate teachers to make changes and avoid the harm caused by maintaining the status quo.

Surfacing the cost of inaction is crucial for school leaders because it helps create a sense of urgency and motivation for change. By making teachers aware of the omission bias and highlighting the potential negative consequences of maintaining the status quo, leaders can create cultures of commitment. By clearly articulating the costs of not changing, such as students not comprehending challenging material, principals can persuade teachers of the necessity of embracing new approaches. They can also help teachers see how new strategies can help them achieve their goals (for example, students understanding the material in their discipline). By surfacing the cost of inaction, the principal in the previous scenario helped teachers see the tangible costs of not addressing literacy challenges.

Collective Impact

When school leaders successfully spark a sense of purpose and garner commitment from their teachers, they unleash the transformative power of collective efficacy. By highlighting achievement gaps, learning from marker students, and surfacing the cost of inaction, principals can inspire their teams to move beyond mere compliance and embrace a shared vision of educational equity and excellence. Efficacy builders can reignite the passion that drew teachers to the profession in the first place: the desire to make a meaningful difference in the lives of every student, regardless of their background or circumstances. Principals can be the catalyst for commitment.

By providing opportunities for teachers to witness the impact of their efforts, leaders will cultivate a culture of commitment, where everyone is motivated in the pursuit of student success. True collective impact is achieved through a shared sense of purpose and a deep belief in the power of collaborative action.

At the compliance end of the spectrum, leaders often plan independently to achieve their goals, avoid ideas that could derail or challenge their agenda, and manage people to ensure they're compliant. School leaders who lean too far toward compliance ultimately build resentment and resistance. Educators feel restricted and innovation is stifled as teams just go through the motions and collective efficacy suffers. An effective efficacy builder can overcome compliance and garner commitment by sparking a sense of purpose. By highlighting a gap, leaders can promote greater commitment. Leaders can also help teachers and teams learn from marker students. As students' needs are met, teacher efficacy is enhanced. Finally, leaders can surface the cost of inaction. Use the exercises and prompts in the reproducible "Planning for Action to Overcome Compliance" (page 52) to practice sparking a sense of purpose to garner greater commitment.

Planning for Action to Overcome Compliance

Use the following exercises to engage with the micro-moves discussed in chapter 3.

Highlighting a Gap

Using a recent set of student achievement data and the following template, input the performance scores across a three-year period to track and monitor growth or decline of performance against the agreed upon standard.

Next, use a filtering tool to disaggregate the data set for the focus group of students (for example, multilingual learners) relevant to your context or improvement efforts.

Finally, calculate the gap over time. What do you notice? Has the gap increased or decreased? What could be the cause? What are the potential solutions?

	Year ____	**Year ____**	**Year ____**	**Gap + or − percent**
Control group				
Focus group (for example, multilingual learners)				

Learning From Marker Students

Select a marker student from your cohort. Review a recent sample of that student's work and identify their learning goals. Bring the marker student's work to the table at a team meeting, collaborate with your team members, and discuss strengths, areas for growth, and strategies to further support their progress.

Next, implement the strategies and report back to the group. What worked? What was still a challenge? What do you still need to adjust?

Finally, continue to track and monitor the marker student's progress over time and evaluate the impact of your teaching. Use the following chart to track the information you gather from your marker student.

Student name: ______________________________

Learning goal: ______________________________

Strengths in sample of work include:	Areas for growth identified in sample of work include:	Next steps and strategies include:	What worked? What was a challenge?	Refine and adjust. Next steps and strategies include:

Surfacing the Cost of Inaction

The following graphic organizer offers a simple way to compare and contrast the status quo against a new approach. Simply add the project name and use the question prompts to stimulate collaborative discussion between what's currently happening (status quo) and potential new approaches that you could take. (Note: these question prompts aren't an exhaustive list. Input the question prompts relevant to your context.)

Project name: ____________________

Question Prompts	Status Quo (Inaction)	New Approach (Action)
What is the evidence of impact on student learning outcomes?	Is our current approach having the desired impact on learning outcomes? How do we know?	If we tried a new approach, would it have a positive impact on learning outcomes? How would we know?
Have we achieved consistent, high-quality implementation?	Does our current approach have consistent, high-quality implementation?	If we tried a new approach, what would high-quality implementation look like?
What are the professional learning opportunities for teaching staff?	What professional learning opportunities support our current ways of working?	What professional learning would we require if we were to try a new approach?

Question Prompts	Status Quo (Inaction)	New Approach (Action)
What are the risks and implications in taking this approach?	What are the risks and implications if we stick with our current approach?	What are the risks and implications if we try a new approach?
What are the costs and resourcing considerations?	What costs and resources are required to sustain our current approach?	What are the costs and resource implications of a new approach?

Part 2

Positive Emotions

Bandura (1998) indicates that people rely partly on their emotional states in judging their capabilities. Individuals associate heightened tensions and anxieties as signs of "vulnerabilities to poor performance" (Bandura, 1998, p. 54). Bandura (1998) also notes that positive moods enhance efficacy. Teachers experiencing positive emotions such as joy, enthusiasm, and satisfaction in their work can bolster their collective belief in their ability to make a difference. These positive affective states can create an upward spiral, where feeling good about their collective efforts leads to even greater confidence and motivation. Bandura (1993) referred to collective efficacy as a renewable resource. In this respect, a team's success in achieving its goals reinforces collective efficacy, which in turn leads to more success and a continued cycle of improvement.

Positive emotions help to build resilience among teachers. Psychologist Barbara L. Fredrickson (2001) explains that certain discrete positive emotions—including joy, interest, contentment, and pride—broaden our perspective and encourage people to explore, learn, and build resources, which in turn help people become more resilient in the face of future challenges. Bandura (2006) also finds that positive emotions can serve as a buffer against the negative effects of stress and setbacks. When teachers maintain positive affective states, even in the face of challenges, they are more likely to persist, adapt, and maintain their collective belief in their ability to succeed. This resilience is crucial for sustaining high levels of collective efficacy.

Furthermore, when a significant number of teachers display positive emotions, it can have a contagious effect throughout the school. Emotions are not just individual experiences but are also social and can be transmitted between people (van Kleef & Côté, 2022). When teachers consistently communicate optimism and encouragement, they can elevate the mood of those around them and this emotional contagion can contribute to a positive school climate and enhance collective efficacy. While emotional contagion can occur naturally, it can also be intentionally cultivated.

By designing environments, interactions, and practices that elevate positivity, principals can create the conditions for positive emotional contagion to flourish.

In the three chapters in part 2, we identify three enemies of efficacy and draw on positivity to overcome these enemies. *Positivity* is a way of thinking and feeling that emphasizes the positive qualities in people, situations, and experiences rather than dwelling on the negative. Key aspects include maintaining a hopeful and confident outlook about the future and focusing on solutions, opportunities, and growth rather than dwelling on problems or limitations. Positivity also involves building and maintaining positive relationships with others. By elevating positivity, principals can create more supportive, resilient, and efficacious environments. A principal can effectively increase positivity as a source of collective efficacy by elevating positive emotions, creating a sense of psychological safety, and prioritizing wellness.

According to Hattie's (2023) Visible Learning synthesis, anxiety has a negative impact on student achievement, with an effect size of −0.40.

In part 2, we discuss the following micro-moves.

- By *labeling emotions*, leaders can extinguish negative emotions and amplify positive ones.
- By *recognizing and celebrating progress*, principals help to create more positive school cultures where teachers feel seen, heard, and appreciated.
- By *leveraging the power of the narrative*, principals increase the likelihood that teachers and students will internalize the belief that they are capable of high standards.
- By *understanding different ways of communicating*, principals can improve the way teachers interact and solve problems together.
- By *modeling collaborative norms*, principals can encourage everyone to contribute their insights and expertise.
- By *sharing feedback*, principals can model vulnerability and build trust, respect, and stronger relationships.

Scholars Megan Tschannen-Moran and Marilyn Barr (2004) refer to collective affective states as the "emotional tone of the organization" (p. 190).

- By *building workplace well-being profiles*, teachers will know that their well-being is being prioritized, which contributes to a more positive culture.
- By *addressing teachers' concerns*, teachers will feel that their concerns are being heard, which reduces stress and anxiety.
- By *increasing interpersonal clarity* in schools, principals deter staff from making up false stories about other staff members without fact checking.

Chapter 4

Positivity Over Negativity

By *elevating positivity*, school leaders can overcome *negativity* as an enemy of efficacy.

In this chapter, we examine how negativity is an enemy of efficacy. To overcome negativity, school leaders must elevate positivity. Three key micro-moves leaders can rely on include labeling emotions, recognizing and celebrating progress, and leveraging the power of the narrative. School leaders achieve collective impact as they prioritize positivity.

Negativity as an Enemy of Efficacy

The power of deficit thinking in a school culture to stifle motivation and effort positions negativity as an enemy of efficacy. When people are prone to negativity they persistently focus on the gloomy aspects of a situation and are pessimistic about the future. Negativity can have a significant impact on educators' well-being and their effectiveness in the classroom. It can contribute to higher levels of stress and burnout (Herman, Hickmon-Rosa, & Reinke, 2018), strained relationships with students and colleagues, and high rates of absenteeism (Bottiani, Duran, Pas, & Bradshaw, 2019). Negativity is therefore an enemy of efficacy.

Negative feelings and emotions are natural. In fact, a review of evidence suggests that bad *is* stronger than good across a broad range of phenomena (Baumeister, Bratslavsky, Finkenauer, & Vohs, 2001). Even for individuals and groups who don't lean into negativity, events that hold negative strength (for example, a production company receives several bad reviews on opening night, a sports team loses a high-stakes game, a sales team fails to meet their quota and misses out on their annual bonus) will have a greater impact than events of the same type that generate positive reaction (for example, getting great reviews, triumphing over your opponent, meeting the sales quota). Bad events produce bigger and longer-lasting effects than good events.

Researchers Roy Baumeister, Ellen Bratslavsky, Catrin Finkenauer, and Kathleen D. Vohs (2001) conducted a review pertaining to the central hypothesis that *bad is stronger than good*. They find that bad events have longer and more intense consequences than good events across several domains. In one example, they cite a study that compared unexpected financial outcomes in scenarios where participants gained or lost the same amount of money. Those who lost money reported greater distress than the joy that accompanied gaining the same amount of money. People had more words for bad emotions than good ones and used them more often. Learning and conditioning were more strongly affected by bad things than good. Bad reputations were easier to acquire than good reputations. At the sensory level, reactions to unpleasant odors were stronger than reactions to pleasant or neutral odors.

Since bad is stronger than good, negative feelings need to be recognized, validated, and addressed. There are often genuine circumstances and experiences that can evoke negativity in schools. However, when a negative tone is pervasive through the school building, collective efficacy becomes challenging to foster and sustain. Equally, we recognize that a culture of toxic positivity can be just as disconcerting. *Toxic positivity* is "the excessive and ineffective overgeneralization of a happy, optimistic state across all situations" (Quintero & Long, n.d.). Psychologists recognize that "the process of toxic positivity results in the denial, minimization, and invalidation of the authentic human emotional experience" (Quintero & Long, n.d.). Sometimes, positivity in the face of an obviously difficult situation can be perceived as insincere and unhelpful.

To realize systemic and sustainable improvement in schools, principals can generate a genuine positive school culture and climate. With careful consideration of word choices, positive dispositions, and solutions-focused mindsets, school leaders can lift efficacy levels. Environments with increased positivity lead to learning and growth. Principals can take intentional steps to overcome negativity as an enemy of efficacy.

Overcome Negativity With Positivity

To counteract a negative school climate, principals can elevate positivity. By emphasizing the power of a positive mindset, school leaders can help teachers understand how their attitudes and beliefs shape their reality. By focusing on positive mindsets, principals can create more supportive and productive school environments. Principals can increase positivity to overcome negativity as an enemy of efficacy.

Positive affective states are an important source of collective efficacy as they influence organizational behavior. Roger D. Goddard, Wayne K. Hoy, and Anita Woolfolk Hoy (2000) share, "efficacious organizations can tolerate pressure and crises and continue to function without severe negative consequences; in fact, they learn how to adapt and to cope with disruptive forces" (p. 484). For schools, the stronger the sense of collective efficacy, the greater the ability to cope with unexpected adverse conditions that may arise. Efficacious schools are positive schools shaped by a determined resolve that they have what it takes to tackle a challenge.

Hoy and colleagues (2002) write that the "strengths or weaknesses of collective efficacy helps or hinders the positive effects of individual efficacy" (p. 82). As a result, stronger collective efficacy encourages individual teachers to more effectively deploy the skills they already have, find new ways to tackle difficult challenges, and share what they know with others. The three micro-moves for elevating positivity in schools include (1) labeling emotions, (2) recognizing and celebrating progress, and (3) leveraging the power of the narrative. These micro-moves can be deployed in a range of different scenarios depending on the context.

Labeling Emotions

Former Federal Bureau of Investigations (FBI) hostage negotiator Chris Voss (2017) provides an effective strategy for overcoming negative emotions in the heat of a situation. Voss, now a worldwide business consultant, honed his skills as a high-stakes negotiator in law enforcement over a number of decades. He used the term *labeling* as a negotiation tactic to diffuse a potentially delicate or tricky situation. Voss (2017) writes, "labeling is a way of validating someone's emotion by acknowledging it" (p. 54). By giving an emotion a name, you're able to identify with how the other person feels, shortcutting your way to an emotional connection. Labeling provides a special advantage as "exposing negative thoughts to daylight makes them seem less frightening" (Voss, 2017, p. 55). Labeling is a simple, versatile skill principals can use to reinforce the positive aspects of a discussion or diffuse the negative ones.

Tapping Into the Sources of Efficacy

Feelings and emotions shape efficacy beliefs. By labeling them, efficacy builders can amplify positive emotions and diminish negative ones.

Emotional states are a key source of collective efficacy and the first step to labeling is to detect the other person's emotional state. The idea is to pay close attention to the person's words, tone, and body language. These clues reveal themselves over the course of a discussion or meeting; you probably will not have any difficulty recalling a time you have seen this unfold in a confrontational meeting. Voss (2017) explains that "once you have identified an emotion you want to highlight," the next step "is to label it aloud. Labels can be phrased as statements or questions" (p. 56).

Voss (2017) notes that the key to an effective label is using a beginning phrase with a neutral statement of understanding. The following are examples of such statements.

- *It seems like* . . . there's some *uncertainty* about this proposal.
- *It sounds like* . . . you could be *worried* about the changes this could cause.
- *It looks like* . . . the strategy is still a little *ambiguous*.

Critically, the statements don't begin with the personal pronoun I. By avoiding I, which makes the statement seemingly about yourself, these statements show you're more interested in understanding the situation and encourage the person to be responsive (Voss, 2017). Once principals have labeled an emotion, the final step is to stay silent. This step is critical as it allows the respondent to share more, revealing further information and providing permission to explore their emotions. The power of labeling is that the label does the heavy lifting.

We have shared the strategy of labeling negative emotions with principals and asked them to try it. When later asked about its effectiveness, one school leader recounted the following.

> A very distraught teacher came into my office last week and was complaining about student misbehavior.
>
> I said to her, "It seems like you're very angry and upset."
>
> She paused for a moment, sat down, and replied, "No, I am just really sad."
>
> I extended an invitation for her to tell me more about how she was feeling, and I could tell that what had weighed heavily on her emotions was starting to lift.
>
> The conversation ended with the teacher identifying some strategies to try to address disobedience. (Participating principal, personal communication, March 12, 2024)

Labeling is an effective micro-move as it identifies negative emotions and diffuses them. Equally, it's useful for enhancing positive emotions and reinforcing them—for example, "*It looks like* you're *motivated* about how this new initiative could unfold." Teasing out negative emotions and bringing them to the surface in a nonconfrontational way acknowledges people's feelings rather than awkwardly avoiding them. This micro-move enhances efficacy; as principals label a negative feeling, they allow it to be discussed and replaced with positive, empathetic, and solutions-based thoughts.

Recognizing and Celebrating Progress

Another efficacy building micro-move is to recognize, acknowledge, and celebrate progress. Instructional leadership teams (ILTs) or collaborative teams provide fertile ground for collective efficacy to develop. An *instructional leadership team* typically includes the principal, assistant principal, instructional coaches, teacher leaders, and other school leaders. These teams provide "powerful levers for making change in schools" and can provide schools with systematic and focused ways of executing their most important priorities (Stricker, 2019). Tschannen-Moran and Barr (2004) identify school principal leadership behaviors as a key to unlocking collective efficacy potential. They share that "in schools with high collective teacher efficacy, principals are instructional leaders who seek creative ways to improve instruction" (p. 195).

ILTs and collaborative teams are perfect platforms for school principals to positively influence the teaching and learning agenda. The beauty of this micro-move is that many schools already have these systems and structures in place. The intent in this micro-move is to focus on positivity by recognizing and celebrating progress and success.

"After people become convinced that they have what it takes to succeed, they persevere in the face of adversity and quickly rebound from setbacks. By sticking it out through the tough times, they emerge from adversity stronger and more able" (Bandura, 1997, p. 80).

Tapping Into the Sources of Efficacy

Recognizing, acknowledging, and celebrating progress are likely to cultivate more positive affective states in a school because doing so boosts the morale of teachers and fosters a collaborative culture where teachers feel valued and appreciated for their contributions. The strategy can strengthen the collective belief in the school's ability to positively impact student outcomes.

Figure 4.1 (page 66) illustrates four simple strategies principals can use to recognize and celebrate progress in an ILT or a collaborative team.

Strategy	Description
Hosting a recognition circle	Add a short recognition circle to the agenda for an ILT. Choose one person at a time to recognize in the group and repeat until everyone has had a turn. The person being recognized simply listens. To make it a bit different, the group can focus words of recognition about a specific topic, like a recent success with student learning or something connected to the school's values.
Starting with strengths	Teams often start meetings by stating a problem of practice and diving into exploring what hasn't been working. Instead, start the next team meeting with what's working well and celebrate that. Acknowledge the strengths and achievements made in the project so far, no matter how small.
Focusing on positive impact	Focus team conversations about the meaning of impact by examining student work samples with impact and evidence of impact in mind. Emphasize positive dialogue, focus on impact-related concerns, and shift thinking away from surface-level issues. This helps teachers realize their actions count. Be socially persuasive and support team members in recognizing they have made the difference.
Boosting efficacy	During ILT and collaborative team meetings, ensure that the positive and credible voices within the school reinforce the stories that capture student success, therefore boosting efficacy. Additionally, ensure that school leaders prepare the dialogue to counter the all-too-common situation when particular individuals in team meetings turn the narrative to the negative. Efficacy is lifted when credible others convey confidence in the team's ability.

Figure 4.1: Micro-moves for recognizing and celebrating progress.

Leveraging the Power of the Narrative

The final micro-move is using the power of our words to shape positive affective states. Jenni Donohoo, John Hattie, and Rachel Eells (2018) write that "the greatest power that principals have in schools is that they can control the narrative of the school" (p. 44). Therefore, a worthwhile challenge is to consider the strategic co-construction of a collective efficacy narrative. Researcher Christine M. Anderson (2022) explains, "A collective efficacy narrative is a story an interdependent group purposely creates about their identity and the significance of the obstacles they have overcome with intention" (p.7). The development of such a narrative is designed to underpin and support the implementation of collective efficacy boosting initiatives. Such a strategy draws on powerful social persuasion and leads to a ripple effect throughout the school.

Tapping Into the Sources of Efficacy

A compelling narrative can shape the overall culture of a school and cultivate a sense of pride, belonging, and positivity among staff, students, and the wider community.

A clear narrative describing the *identity* of the group is key. Teachers and students need to see themselves positively overcoming obstacles within the narrative. The narrative must detail the type of learning and learning behaviors that are valued at the school, helping to crystallize in people's minds how things work around here and what really matters.

Anderson (2022) advises that "compelling collective efficacy narratives are not authentically crafted in isolation" (p. 10). She also notes it's important that narratives are "co-constructed by listening to teachers share their stories and by interlacing narratives with reflections on collective experiences and practices" (Anderson, 2022, p. 10). Anderson's insights underscore the importance of actively involving teams of teachers in the narrative-building process. By doing so, they tap into the wealth of experiences and perspectives among their faculty. The consultative approach to creating a collective teacher narrative also gives the team a sense of agency.

This is a helpful strategy to build trust and belief. By involving teachers in the process of crafting collective efficacy narratives, school leaders demonstrate transparency. This openness helps break down hierarchical barriers and shows that leadership values the input and experiences of all team members. When people feel that leadership is not hiding things from them and is seeking their opinions, it naturally fosters trust.

Also, when teachers share their stories and see those stories reflected in the collective narrative, it validates their experiences. This validation communicates that their perspectives are valued and important, which can significantly boost their belief in the organization and its leadership. The co-construction component of the strategy empowers teachers, leaders, and students to share their positive stories where they have overcome difficulties and persisted in the face of challenges. Processing past experiences in a supportive, socially persuasive environment helps to reaffirm team efforts and reinforces an attitude of "We've got this!" Leaders and teachers can achieve this by investing time together, authentically shaping the narrative for the school by clearly defining what's important, describing how the team wants to represent itself, and most importantly, how team members see themselves working for the students.

Given the significance of positivity in fostering collective efficacy, this micro-move is simple and strategic. Rather than efficacy becoming diminished through the underlying narrative, a compellingly crafted story can reinforce a stronger sense of efficacy. Principals can use the power of a positive narrative to support efficacy levels at both a whole-school and team level.

Goddard and colleagues (2000) write, "To the extent *collective teacher efficacy* is *positively associated* with *student achievement*, there is strong reason to lead schools in a direction that will systematically develop teacher efficacy; such efforts may indeed be rewarded with continuous growth in not only collective teacher efficacy but also in student achievement" (p. 483, emphasis added).

Collective Impact

When school leaders successfully elevate positivity and overcome the pervasive influence of negativity, they create an environment where collective efficacy can flourish. By skillfully labeling emotions, recognizing and celebrating progress, and leveraging the power of a compelling narrative, principals can transform the affective state of their school community. School leaders have the power to shape the emotional landscape of their teams, inspiring them to approach challenges with optimism, resilience, and a steadfast belief in their collective ability to make a difference. By consistently modeling and reinforcing a positive mindset, effective efficacy builders will cultivate a culture where teachers feel supported, empowered, and motivated. Together, school leaders and teachers have the power to create brighter futures for students—one positive step at a time. Collective impact is possible when positive words, dispositions, and mindsets influence collective efficacy.

Negativity is an enemy of efficacy because it spreads quickly through a team or entire faculty, results in low morale, and—in the worst case—produces toxic school cultures. Rachel Eells (2011) writes, "highly efficacious teams or individuals will feel optimistic about success because they feel that they have the abilities needed to create that success" (p. 5). With positive thinking, educators see limitations as challenges rather than roadblocks, and they assess uncontrolled circumstances for what they can control. The affective state of a school has a lot to do with how staff assess and confront challenges. Leaders' behaviors play a key role in guiding their schools to influence these assessments in either positive or negative ways. An effective efficacy builder can overcome negativity by applying the micro-moves outlined in this chapter, including labeling emotions, recognizing and celebrating progress, and leveraging the power of the narrative. Use the exercises and prompts in the reproducible "Planning for Action to Overcome Negativity" (page 70) to practice prioritizing positivity.

Planning for Action to Overcome Negativity

Use the following exercises to engage with the micro-moves discussed in chapter 4.

Labeling Emotions

Reflect on a conversation or a meeting you've had recently. Think about moments when you could have labeled emotions and write down some examples of what you could have said.

- It seems like . . . ______________________________
- It sounds like . . . ______________________________
- It looks like . . . ______________________________

Reflect on your notes in preparation for future meetings.

Recognizing and Celebrating Success

In figure 4.1 (page 66), you saw an example of how to use micro-moves to recognize and celebrate progress. Now try using this tool in your context. Use the following template to prepare for your next instructional leadership team or collaborative team meeting to recognize and celebrate successes.

Hosting a recognition circle	What is a theme (for example, positive team communication) you would like to use for your recognition circle?
Starting with strengths	What strengths do you need to recognize? What deserves celebration?
Focusing on positive impact	What's a positive piece of student evidence that shows a deliberate strategy has achieved a positive impact?
Efficacy boosters	Who are the credible sources that can encourage the team and boost efficacy?

Leveraging the Power of the Narrative

As a team, in one hundred words or less, describe your collective efficacy narrative. Be clear and succinct as you answer the following questions: How will you grow collective efficacy within your school? What obstacles will you overcome? How will people see themselves within the narrative?

Chapter 5

Psychological Safety Over Judgment

By *enhancing psychological safety*, school leaders can overcome *judgment* as an enemy of efficacy.

In this chapter, we explore how judgment becomes an enemy of efficacy. School leaders can overcome judgment by promoting a psychologically safe environment. Three key micro-moves leaders can turn to include understanding different ways of communicating, modeling the norms of collaboration, and sharing feedback. School leaders achieve collective impact as they overcome judgment by enhancing psychological safety.

Judgment as an Enemy of Efficacy

Collective efficacy is measured as a judgment made by group members about the group. When those judgments are positive, collective efficacy is high. However, when group members judge the collective as not being able to make a real difference, collective efficacy is diminished. Researchers Curt M. Adams and Patrick B. Forsyth (2006) highlight this notion by noting, "Individuals within organizations make judgments, based on past experiences and contextual circumstances, about the collective ability of the organization to perform future tasks that will affect goal obtainment" (p. 631). These "judgments form the basis of organizational agency, which influences perceptions, behavior and actions of an organization" (Adams & Forsyth, 2006, p. 631). If educators experience an enemy of efficacy and don't act to overcome it, the result can limit the potential to cultivate collective efficacy and affect the sense of collective agency. Our judgments have a significant impact on our behaviors and actions, so it's important to consider how we can influence them.

Goddard and colleagues (2000) identify judgment as being a critical element to the formation of efficacy beliefs. Their model suggests that the four sources of efficacy are processed through two key elements in the development of collective efficacy: (1) analysis of the teaching task and (2) assessment of teaching competence. In analyzing the teaching task, teachers judge "what constitutes successful teaching in their school, what barriers or limitations must be overcome, and what resources are available to achieve success" (Goddard et al., 2000, p. 485). As explained in chapter 2 (page 27), when teachers judge the task as too difficult (that is, the magnitude of the task is too great), collective efficacy is impacted.

"The stronger the beliefs people hold about their collective capabilities, the more they achieve" (Bandura, 1997, p. 480).

In the second element of developing collective efficacy, teachers analyze the teaching task in conjunction with the teaching competence within the building. Goddard and colleagues (2000) explain that "teachers make explicit judgments of the teaching competence of their colleagues in light of an analysis of the teaching task in their specific school" (p. 485). The challenge for an efficacy leader is to create the culture where colleagues build confidence in their competences together—as a team. Making judgments is an inescapable component of collective efficacy. An effective efficacy builder will ensure that judgments are made that cultivate rather than hinder collective efficacy.

Judgment not only occurs at the whole-school level, but also presents at the team and individual level. Jumping to conclusions, making assumptions, or passing judgment about team members are all forms of making judgment. These work in both positive and negative ways and impact individual and team performance. The challenge with judgment is that it is sometimes truly hard to detect. People can hide their true feelings by saying one thing to the group but thinking and doing another. Silence is also a form of judgment. Team members who stay silent give the pretense of agreement but may not really be on board at all. Finally, judgment can create friction within a team. For these reasons, judgment is an enemy of efficacy. Table 5.1 (page 75) illustrates how judgments affect efficacy.

Table 5.1: Judgments About Collective Efficacy

Judgment Enhancing Efficacy	Judgment Diminishing Efficacy
• My team *works well* together, challenging each other's thoughts in a respectful way. • My team leader has a *high degree of credibility* through the knowledge she shares. • I believe that teachers in this school *can really get through to* the most difficult students. • I'm *confident in my colleagues* that we can work it out together.	• My team members just *don't really understand* this assessment task. • Our team leaders *just don't know* what they're talking about. • The *lack of instructional materials and outdated resources* in this school makes teaching very difficult. • Administration has *no idea about the pressure we're facing*. They're out of touch.

While ILTs and collaborative team meetings provide excellent structures for building collective efficacy, they can also erode trust if negative judgments impact team members. If led poorly, teachers will become reluctant to fully share their knowledge with their team or to take risks in their teaching for fear of being judged. It tends to make people more isolated (discussed in chapter 10, page 151) and leads them to operate as individuals rather than collaborate toward a shared goal.

When they detect judgment, teachers may not feel comfortable sharing problems. They may remain silent and feel alone. Rather than encouraging teachers to share and trust the team to help solve problems together, judgments can erode trust and affect the team's ability to achieve their shared purpose. In addition, teachers may come to view classroom visits involving other teachers and administrators as criticism rather than as a supportive learning opportunity. To capitalize on the impact of these structures, principals need to be mindful to ensure they remain judgment-free zones. In these settings, creating psychologically safe spaces where teamwork can flourish is paramount.

To realize improvement in schools, principals can create and reinforce cultures where judgment does not cloud efficacy. Leaders can capitalize on positive emotions and construct environments where teamwork is promoted, ideas flow, and risk taking is encouraged. Principals can take intentional steps to enhance psychological safety to overcome judgment as an enemy of efficacy.

Overcome Judgment With Psychological Safety

School principals can counteract judgment and strengthen efficacy by creating psychologically safe teams. In the quest to build the perfect team, Google conducted a study starting in 2012 called Project Aristotle in which the company explored half a century's worth of research on team functioning and deeply examined hundreds of teams to determine their answer. One key discovery was that it didn't matter so much who was on the team, but how team members were able to understand and be influenced by group norms (Duhigg, 2016). As their research progressed, one important group norm shone through more than others as the most important ingredient in developing the perfect team: psychological safety. School leaders can create psychological safety to overcome judgment as an enemy of efficacy.

Coined by leadership and teaming scholar Amy C. Edmondson (2019), the term *team psychological safety* is broadly defined as "a climate in which people are comfortable expressing and being themselves" (p. xvi). In the school environment, this type of climate is critical for cultivating collective efficacy. Edmondson (2019) writes, "when people have psychological safety at work, they feel comfortable sharing concerns and mistakes without fear of embarrassment or retribution" (p. xvi). When teams are working in a climate of psychological safety, the impact of negative judgments is mitigated. Team members become confident they can share their thoughts without being humiliated, blamed, or ignored.

When a controversial issue is put on the table, efficacious teams with high levels of psychological safety cast judgment aside for the greater good of the team. This allows them to fully discuss the issue and promote creative and innovative thinking when determining a solution. Without judgment or criticism, team members know they can ask questions when they are uncertain, forming tighter connections with their teammates. In a psychologically safe zone, team members are more likely to develop trust and respect with their colleagues. In addition, when mistakes do happen, they are likely to be reported quickly so prompt corrective action can be taken.

Psychological safety doesn't happen by chance. In his research on the concept, social scientist Timothy R. Clark (2020) defines four successive stages that teams work through in developing an environment where employees feel included, are fully engaged, and are encouraged to contribute their best efforts and ideas. Clark (2020) defines the four stages of psychological safety as follows.

1. **Inclusion Safety:** This is the stage when you feel safe to be yourself and feel a sense of belonging to the team. This satisfies the need to feel accepted and is viewed as a moral imperative.
2. **Learner Safety:** This stage allows us to feel safe as we engage in all aspects of the learning process, even making mistakes. This satisfies the need to learn and grow and is important to develop self-efficacy.
3. **Contributor Safety:** This stage is where you feel safe to use your talents and skills to make a difference as a fully-fledged member of the team.

When leaders create a sense of contributor safety for others, we empower them with autonomy and encouragement.

4. **Challenger Safety:** This is the stage when you feel you're able to question or challenge the status quo if you believe things can improve without worrying that something will be held against you. This stage satisfies the need to make things better and allows you to showcase your creativity.

Clark (2020) summarizes the concept in this way: "psychological safety is a condition in which you feel (1) included, (2) safe to learn, (3) safe to contribute, and (4) safe to challenge the status quo—all without fear of being embarrassed, marginalized, or punished in some way" (p. 2).

Leaders of efficacy will be aware of the importance of psychological safety in their teams. They will be aware of how to minimize the efficacy-diminishing effects of judgment and promote a psychologically safe climate. Three micro-moves that principals can use to promote psychological safety include (1) understanding different ways of communicating, (2) modeling the norms of collaboration, and (3) sharing feedback.

In the article "A Guide to Building Psychological Safety on Your Team," Rakshitha Arni Ravishankar (2022) shares a key strategy: "Embrace different communication styles: Instead of forcing people to stick to specific ways of communication, let them articulate themselves in a way that feels more authentic to them."

Understanding Different Ways of Communicating

An ideal starting point in building a sense of psychological safety is understanding the different ways in which people communicate. Establishing clear lines of communication helps team dynamics and is a practical way of building trust. One method to build an understanding of different ways of communicating is a team protocol activity with safe but focused questions to determine how the team likes to communicate, how they work together, and the things they value in their work. Establishing the ways people like to communicate is an effective way to suspend judgment as team members come to know, learn about, and accept differences with their teammates' working styles.

For optimal results, teams would complete this type of activity at the starting point of a project, the beginning of a new school year, or when a new team is formed. The facilitator plays a crucial role in setting the scene and creating a climate where people feel safe to share. Edmondson (2019) explains, "leaders who explicitly ask for team members' input are likely to encourage team psychological safety" (p. 16). It's important that leaders model the way by encouraging input and demonstrating that it's OK to have different preferences. Further, facilitators of this activity would display courage and vulnerability by showing acceptance of each team member's different preferences.

Tapping Into the Sources of Efficacy

When team members feel psychologically safe and understood, they are more likely to engage in open and honest dialogue. This can lead to a more positive and constructive exchange of ideas, feedback, and support, which can contribute to overall positive affective states within the school.

Figure 5.1 (page 79) illustrates a team protocol activity in which each team member creates their own personal guide to how they like to work and then shares their guide with the team. The activity provides scope for a response in three areas: communication style, working style, and deeper connections. The facilitator guides each participant to share their responses and, importantly, demonstrates vulnerability to ensure team members feel safe to share. You can access a template of the protocol in the reproducible "Planning for Action to Overcome Judgment" (page 84) at the end of this chapter.

Tapping Into the Sources of Efficacy

Miscommunication and misunderstandings can be significant sources of stress and anxiety in the workplace. By establishing clear lines of communication and understanding different communication styles, schools can reduce these negative affective states and promote a more positive and supportive work environment.

Establishing team protocols is an effective way of building awareness of the different personalities within the team. Differentiating meeting structures helps to create psychological safety.

Area for Response	Instructions	Takeaways
Communication style	Team members identify the ways they like to communicate. Then they share the following. • Their preferred communication methods (for example, in person, email, messaging, or phone) • How they prefer to receive constructive feedback (for example, straight and direct, direct but with some context, or direct but with some processing time) • What format works best for them (for example, individually, in a small group, or in a large group)	This information is critical for leaders so they can differentiate team tasks to suit communication styles. In addition, it's useful information to consider during reflection sessions, as leaders can provide feedback to the team in a way that suits members' expressed style.
Working style	Team members share their preferred working style. Some team members may feel they work best alone, others in a large group setting.	This activity will provide useful information to guide future work tasks. When team members feel they have been heard and had their preferences recognized, they're likely to have a greater sense of trust in their teammates. A strategic leader will use this information to engage the strengths of their team.
Deeper connection	The team explores topics related to personal values and trust. Team members share what they value, what may have frustrated them in the past, and what they see as being a key ingredient for an effective team.	Going deeper allows teams to initiate the connections that will be beneficial when the going gets tough. Knowing the core values of team members and understanding what makes them tick will be helpful to collective efficacy builders.

Figure 5.1: Team protocol activity.

Visit **go.SolutionTree.com/teacherefficacy** *for a free reproducible of this figure.*

According to Hattie's (2023) Visible Learning synthesis, teacher collaboration has an effect size (ES) of 0.38. You might wonder why we would call out the fact that the effect of collaboration is below the "hinge point." Hattie (2023) explains the significance of the hinge point (ES = 0.40) as the average of all the influences, representing a year's worth of progress for the year spent in school. A common misperception is that if an influence is below the hinge point, school leaders should not focus their efforts on it. However, the effect sizes reported in Hattie's meta-analysis demonstrate what *currently is*—not what *could be.* If collaboration were strengthened in schools, (and our experience tells us there is plenty of room for improvements), the effect size would increase significantly. Also, an effect size of 0.38 is fairly significant.

Modeling the Norms of Collaboration

Collaboration is an important concept for collective efficacy. Researchers Kerry Elliott and Hilary Hollingsworth (2020) state, "Even though collaboration is vital to developing collective efficacy, and collective efficacy implies that teachers who work together and believe they can make a difference will improve student outcomes, it is actually more complicated than that" (p. 33). The complicated aspect of collaboration is ensuring that it actually meets the intended purpose and in such a way that it promotes positive working relationships. It's relatively simple to put teams of teachers together, but it's more complex to ensure those teams generate the desired outcomes.

Tapping Into the Sources of Efficacy

When teachers demonstrate norms of collaboration including active listening and respectful communication, it fosters a sense of belonging and support among colleagues. Feeling part of a supportive team can boost morale and positive emotions.

An effective approach to ensuring that collaboration meets the intended purpose is modeling collaboration norms. *Norms* are the agreed protocols for how the team works. Jenni Donohoo and Moses Velasco (2016) write that norms "are initially explicit and verbalized but eventually become cultural (unsaid but understood) expectations of how individuals on the team should conduct themselves" (p. 89). Defining the norms of collaboration goes a long way to building psychological safety as teams take comfort in the safety of the process and come to know what to expect in collaborative settings.

Three norms for collaboration that promote psychological safety include (1) inviting all voices to be heard, (2) suspending judgment and increasing curiosity, and (3) responding productively. We detail these norms in the following section.

- **Inviting all voices to be heard:** During collaborative meetings, principals will ensure all participants have the chance to contribute, whether verbally or in writing. Establishing a framework to ensure each participant can contribute shows the importance of a contribution from everyone. Each voice matters. Collective impact is harnessing the impact of the collective. With all voices heard, the sense of psychological safety grows. When each voice is heard, disgruntled team members are less inclined for to share their voices following the meeting.

- **Suspending judgment and increasing curiosity:** This norm is critical for collaboration. When presented with key information, new data, or a different point of view, the first step is not to judge, but to become curious. This involves spending time creating questions and wondering—either individually or as a collective group. The advantage of this approach allows team members to broaden their perspectives, think laterally, and seek more information rather than immediately making a judgment.
- **Responding productively:** The final norm for collaboration is to respond productively. In this norm, the team reaches agreement on the next step following the meeting. Having clarity and consensus will help generate momentum toward the shared goals.

This micro-move captures some simple strategies for collaboration. Initially, norms may be stated explicitly at the beginning of team meetings; however, over time, they will become the understood ways of working.

Sharing Feedback

Researchers Constantinos G. V. Coutifaris and Adam M. Grant (2022) note that "although scholars have highlighted the benefits of psychological safety, relatively few studies have examined how leaders establish it" (p. 1574). Coutifaris and Grant (2022) highlight the concept of feedback sharing to promote long-term psychological safety and made a distinction between feedback sharing and feedback seeking. *Feedback seeking* happens when leaders make "a direct request for information on how to improve" (Coutifaris & Grant, 2022, p. 1575). This is the typical advice given to those in leadership positions. Leaders are

Writer, teacher, and speaker Margaret J. Wheatley (2002) writes, "When we listen with less judgment, we always develop better relationships with each other. It's not differences that divide us. It's our judgments about each other that do. Curiosity and good listening bring us back together" (p. 40).

often encouraged to seek feedback about their performance to demonstrate their willingness to learn and establish trust. In their experimental study, however, Coutifaris and Grant (2022) found that while feedback seeking had a short-lived effect on psychological safety, it wasn't sustained over the long term.

Through qualitative interviews, Coutifaris and Grant (2022) shed some light on why psychological safety, through feedback seeking, was not sustained in the organizations they studied. They learned that when leaders sought feedback, initially employees took it "as a sign of openness and worth and spoke up" (Coutifaris & Grant, 2022, p. 1589). However, some leaders responded defensively, some found the feedback useless, and some felt helpless to address it. Because the leaders did not "provide direction on what type of feedback would be beneficial, employees often commented on areas that were not important or beyond their spans of control" (p. 1590).

Coutifaris and Grant (2022) find that the sense of futility resulting on the part of both leaders and employees decreased their motivation to continue seeking and giving feedback. Vulnerability dissolved as leaders responded defensively or did not take action on the suggestions. Feedback seeking "did not appear to build psychological safety through strengthening trust between leaders and followers" (p. 1590).

Tapping Into the Sources of Efficacy

Sharing feedback can boost positive affective states in a school by normalizing vulnerability and building psychological safety. Coutifaris and Grant (2022) explain, "Seeking feedback created a wide funnel that invited comments and suggestions on a wide range of issues, undermining the efficacy of both leaders and employees" (p. 1593). By openly discussing criticisms and suggestions, leaders reduce uncertainty about what issues are safe to raise, fostering a more open and supportive environment where students and staff feel comfortable expressing themselves.

What did have an enduring effect on psychological safety was leaders sharing feedback. *Feedback sharing* involved "disclosing suggestions for improvement that one has received in the past" (Coutifaris & Grant, 2022, p. 1575). Leaders sharing feedback they had previously received and openly discussing criticisms and suggestions on improving their past performance, helped to "normalize vulnerability" (p. 1586). Coutifaris and Grant (2022) determine that engaging in feedback sharing did not jeopardize leaders' reputations as effective and competent. Rather, feedback sharing demonstrated that leaders could handle criticism, acknowledge their limitations, establish trustworthiness, and reduce uncertainty about what issues were safe to raise. With practice, leaders felt more comfortable opening up and employees felt more comfortable speaking up. Coutifaris and Grant's (2022) study reports that "acts of feedback sharing were often met with crickets in the room" (p. 1586) but over time, as leaders made public commitments to keep sharing and employees reciprocated, it "opened the door for more actionable feedback, greater accountability, and ongoing practices that allowed psychological safety to endure" (p. 1574).

Collective Impact

When school leaders successfully foster psychological safety and overcome the detrimental effects of judgment, they create an environment where collective efficacy can thrive. By taking the time to understand different communication styles, model the norms of collaboration, and courageously share feedback, principals can cultivate a culture of trust, vulnerability, and continuous growth. School leaders have the power to set the tone for their teams, encouraging them to bring their authentic selves to the table and contribute their unique perspectives and ideas without fear of retribution or embarrassment. When principals consistently demonstrate their own willingness to learn, grow, and acknowledge limitations, they inspire their teachers to do the same. Psychological safety is the foundation on which teachers can take risks, challenge the status quo, and work together to achieve extraordinary results for their students. Greater impact is realized when judgment is replaced by curiosity, defensiveness is replaced by openness, and collective efficacy drives transformative change for all learners.

"Sharing feedback created a filter, helping employees to concentrate on issues that were important and controllable for leaders" (Coutifaris & Grant, 2022, p. 1593).

Judgment is an enemy of efficacy because it negatively impacts psychological safety within the team. When team members feel judged, they hide their true selves. As a result, they're less likely to feel they can develop the trust needed for high levels of collective efficacy. An effective efficacy builder can overcome judgment by fostering the conditions that promote psychological safety. By progressively working through the stages of psychological safety, leaders can create spaces where all team members give full input into solving complex challenges. The micro-moves in this chapter include understanding different ways of communicating, modeling the norms of collaboration, and sharing feedback. Use the exercises and prompts in the reproducible "Planning for Action to Overcome Judgment" (page 84) to practice building psychologically safe teams.

Planning for Action to Overcome Judgment

Use the following exercises to engage with the micro-moves discussed in chapter 5.

Team Protocol Activity

Using the following team protocol activity template, ask each member of your team to complete the questions in each section. Once completed, share as a group.

Communication style

- What are my favorite modes of communication?
- When do I do my best work?
- Where do I like to work?
- How do I like to receive feedback?

Working style

- I like to work best on (circle an option)

One project at a time	A small number of things	Many things at once

- I prefer to work (circle an option)

Alone	In a small team	As part of a larger group

- The best time for me to work is (circle an option)

Early morning	Through the day	I'm a night owl

- When I'm working (circle an option)

Don't disrupt me at all	Some disruptions are OK	I can multitask without losing focus

Deeper connections

- What are three values important to me?

- What are three things I value in my colleagues?

- What is something I find frustrating at work?

- What is important to me when building a relationship?

Norms for Collaboration

List the agreed-on norms for collaboration for your context. Importantly, allow the team to be involved in creating the norms.

Norms for Collaboration	Our Norms
Norms for ensuring all voices are heard	
Norms for suspending judgment and increasing curiosity	
Norms for responding productively	
Other norms for collaboration	

Sharing Feedback

Identify a few instances in which you received helpful feedback. What were you trying to improve? What were the suggestions for improvement?

Who will you share this information with and what feedback will you solicit from them as you do so?

Chapter 6

Well-Being Over Uncertainty

By *prioritizing well-being*, school leaders can overcome *uncertainty* as an enemy of efficacy.

In this chapter, we discuss how uncertainty becomes an enemy of efficacy. School leaders can overcome uncertainty by prioritizing well-being. Three key micro-moves leaders can use include building workplace well-being profiles, addressing teachers' concerns, and increasing interpersonal clarity. School leaders achieve collective impact as they overcome uncertainty and support teachers' well-being.

Uncertainty as an Enemy of Efficacy

One component of the well-known acronym *VUCA* (volatility, uncertainty, complexity, and ambiguity) is the term *uncertainty*. The United States Army War College introduced the VUCA acronym by in the late 1980s to describe the volatile, uncertain, complex, and ambiguous nature of the world after the Cold War. The concept has since gained broader use in business, leadership, and education (Bennett & Lemoine, 2014). In this chapter, we introduce the concept of uncertainty as an enemy of efficacy.

Uncertainty has been demonstrated to have negative outcomes on behavior, cognition, and affect. In their behavioral study, researchers Adrian R. Walker, Danielle J. Navarro, Ben R. Newell, and Tom Beesley (2022) demonstrate that unexpected uncertainty plays a key role in people's reactions, causing them to change their behaviors even when they would have been better off sticking with current strategies. Psychology researchers Dan W. Grupe and Jack B. Nitschke (2013) show that uncertainty disrupts many automatic cognitive processes that govern routine action. And finally, researchers Jayne Morriss, Kimberly Goh, Colette R. Hirsch, and Helen F. Dodd (2023) demonstrate that uncertainty heightens existing negative emotional

As Bandura (2000) states, negative emotions diminish efficacy and positive emotions strengthen it. Researchers Carrie D. Allen and William R. Penuel (2015) have uncovered some additional sources of teachers' uncertainty, including conflicting goals, absence of measures, limited resources, and role ambiguity.

Research shows distinctive patterns between perceived uncertainty and a lack of collective teacher efficacy (Schechter & Qadach, 2012). When teachers were uncertain why decisions were made in schools and school districts, it weakened their efficacy.

states and dampens existing positive emotional states. When a situation is uncertain, it impacts people's brains, filling their bodies with anxious emotional energy.

Anxious emotional energy that results from uncertainty can affect school staff. From a school or system leadership perspective, uncertainty is an enemy of efficacy because it hinders the ability to reach consensus on goals. Uncertainty at the strategic level can ripple into collaborative teams, causing educators to be unclear about how to prioritize their work and subsequently reach agreement on their actionable next steps.

In our experiences, two common causes of uncertainty are changes in school leadership (that is, a new principal or assistant principal in the building) and changes in school policies or programs (that is, the introduction of new curriculum, initiatives, or schedules). Progress is stifled and productivity is impacted when educators are not sure of what changes might be around the next corner. When faced with the uncertainty caused by changes like these, teachers grow concerned about what will be expected of them and how they might manage change as part of their daily routines.

When a new principal arrives at the building, it's natural for teachers to feel a sense of uncertainty as new ways of working are established, priorities are reformed, and the new platform for school improvement is set. We're sure you can relate to stories of a new principal arriving, turning the school program upside down, and then dealing with years of fallout. This dynamic fractures relationships, creates uncertainty, and forms an us-versus-them culture. This is the exact opposite of our intent in building strong levels of collective efficacy. If feelings of uncertainty when there's a change in leadership are not navigated strategically, collective efficacy can become at risk.

When changes in a program occur, such as the introduction of a new curriculum, uncertainty rises and impacts teachers' well-being by causing them to stress or worry. Adapting to new policies or programs requires teachers to step out of their comfort zones and change their established routines. This uncertainty about how the changes will impact their teaching and students can cause stress and anxiety. Implementing new policies or programs often involves additional planning, preparation, and professional learning. Teachers may worry about how they will manage their time effectively to balance these new responsibilities with their existing workload. Furthermore, teachers may feel stressed if they believe they lack the necessary support, resources, or training to implement new policies or programs effectively. Also, if the new policy or program conflicts with a teacher's teaching philosophy or professional judgment, they may experience cognitive dissonance and emotional stress. For these reasons, uncertainty is an enemy of efficacy.

"The arrival of a new principal often signals a period of uncertainty and transition for schools. Both faculty and parents may be unclear about the new leader's expectations, priorities, and strategies for change. This ambiguity can fuel anxiety, erode trust, and stall progress until the principal's vision becomes clear and stakeholders develop confidence in the new administration" (Leithwood, Louis, Anderson, & Wahlstrom, 2004, p. 24).

Another way that uncertainty puts efficacy at risk is that educators aren't always clear on the reasons why their colleagues are doing what they are doing or saying what they are saying. There is always an amount of uncertainty regarding other people's experiences (what they are thinking, feeling, or wanting). Leadership and organization scholar Gervase R. Bushe (2010) notes that uncertainty regarding others' motives creates anxiety and people start to make up stories to fill in the gaps in their knowledge. Consider the negative emotions that are likely to result from stories made up to explain other people's behavior.

- Greg's parents scheduled a parent-teacher conference because they wanted to challenge me on the grade he was assigned. (The teacher might feel defensive, annoyed, or bitter.)
- The school principal walked right past me and ignored me. Someone must have told her that I complained about the new supervision schedule. (The teacher might feel anxious, embarrassed, or nervous.)
- The librarian's decision to cancel our library period at the last minute is because she is unprepared and lazy. (The teacher might feel irritated, taken advantage of, or overwhelmed.)

- My teaching partner is unreceptive to my ideas on using manipulatives in mathematics because she didn't respond to my email. (The teacher might feel disappointed, rejected, or angry.)

Psychology professor Frank C. Keil (2006) conducted a review about how people make sense of others' behavior and experiences and explained that they generate explanations based on their existing knowledge and assumptions. Keil argues that the process of explanation-based sense making is a fundamental aspect of human cognition, but it can also lead to biased or incomplete understanding when the assumptions are not checked against reality.

In these examples, there are many unchecked assumptions. Bushe (2010) refers to unchecked assumptions as "interpersonal mush" and notes the "unfortunate truth that the stories we make up, and the stories that get made up about us, tend to be more unfavorable than the reality" (p. 29). When people can't tolerate uncertainty, it causes problems because it is a major fuel for worry and often results in people inventing stories as they try to make sense of things. It is for this reason as well that uncertainty is an enemy of efficacy.

To realize systemic and sustainable improvement in schools, principals can create cultures of well-being to help overcome the negative effects of uncertainty. Leaders can promote positivity to reduce stress, burnout, and turnover. Such environments that prioritize well-being lead to learning and growth. System and school leaders can take intentional steps to overcome uncertainty as an enemy of efficacy.

Overcome Uncertainty With Well-Being

School leaders can overcome uncertainty by prioritizing teacher well-being. Teachers with strong well-being are often more adaptable to change and willing to try new strategies in the classroom. This flexibility and openness to growth can lead to an increased sense of efficacy as they discover new ways to support student learning. Furthermore, when teachers feel valued, respected, and cared for, they are more likely to collaborate, innovate, and contribute to a supportive and inclusive school environment. School leaders can prioritize wellness to ensure uncertainty does not diminish collective efficacy.

Teacher well-being expert Amy Green (2022) highlights the importance of reducing uncertainty by creating positive workplace well-being. Through her Teacher Well-Being Framework, Green (2022) identifies building collective efficacy as a critical component of workplace well-being and a key feature of a positive and healthy workplace. Green (2022) views *everyday well-being*, which she defines as our "energy and function, resilience, and emotional regulation" (p. 26), and *workplace well-being* as equally important parts of building teacher well-being and realizing the true potential of the educators in our schools.

In her framework, Green (2022) shares that, "engagement, productivity and performance and growth are indicators of high workplace well-being" (p. 40), with each of these separate but interrelated elements critically important to increasing wellness. When there are high levels of well-being, school staff are more likely to enjoy their work, become more efficient, increase their levels of productivity, and commit to increased levels of performance. The key is for school principals to be mindful of these components in their planning.

School leaders and teachers play an important role in increasing well-being. Both teachers and principals alike must be alert to the needs of teachers and respond flexibly when situations arise without prior notice. As Green (2022) states, "A leadership team's main priority should be identifying where stress or friction is occurring and trying to reduce this as quickly as possible so (teacher) engagement can rise" (p. 42). These messages are important when navigating periods of uncertainty, slicing through the ambiguity to boost efficacy levels. The following micro-moves can be used as proactive and protective factors to ensure well-being and collective efficacy remain high even through a change of school leadership or programs and policies. Three micro-moves for prioritizing well-being include (1) building workplace well-being profiles, (2) addressing teachers' concerns, and (3) increasing interpersonal clarity.

Building Workplace Well-Being Profiles

The first leadership micro-move for reducing uncertainty is creating workplace well-being profiles. A *workplace well-being profile* is an activity that helps teachers reflect upon, identify, and document their sense of engagement, productivity, and performance and growth. Principals can use this information as a proactive and supportive strategy, rather than being reactive when uncertainty has already had a negative impact. Green (2022) identifies three priorities for workplace well-being.

1. **Engagement:** The teacher enjoys their work, works with a sense of autonomy and purpose, and has positive relationships with others.
2. **Productivity:** The teacher can work efficiently in a given time frame to achieve an output.
3. **Performance and growth:** The teacher is open and willing to discuss, share, and seek feedback and reflect on their performance of practice.

School leaders initiate the process of building workplace well-being profiles by asking teachers to provide information for each of the well-being priorities (engagement, productivity, and performance and growth) using a Likert scale (from a low of 1 to a high of 5). This self-analysis gives educators a starting point to explore their levels of workplace well-being. The leadership team then collects and analyzes this baseline data to create a summary of workplace well-being levels across the school.

Creating workplace well-being profiles assists principals in understanding the trigger points when teachers' well-being needs could be in jeopardy. Feelings of uncertainty are sometimes unavoidable. This micro-move provides a starting point for the conversation about workplace well-being by opening the dialogue and creating a baseline data set. Most importantly, workplace well-being profiles can help principals gain clarity about teachers' experiences and help reduce interpersonal mush. When school leaders gain a better understanding of teachers' perceptions of their engagement, productivity, and performance and growth, they can better understand teachers' experiences. This will help reduce the need to create stories to fill in the blanks about what teachers are thinking, feeling, and wanting. The less interpersonal mush in an organization, the healthier the organization will be.

Tapping Into the Sources of Efficacy

Building workplace well-being profiles can help increase positive feelings in schools by providing a starting point for conversations about well-being. By gaining a better understanding of teachers' perceptions of their engagement, productivity, performance, and growth, principals can reduce interpersonal mush and create a healthier organization.

The leadership team must recognize that collecting data is just the beginning. Once they have captured this data snapshot, they must take action based on the insights it provides. From a school leadership perspective, if educators' engagement scores are lower than expected, leaders may need to clarify the vision, increase positive recognition, or regroup and reform the norms for collaboration. If productivity is waning, it could be time to explore the school systems and structures for working together. Low productivity may be a result of too many layers of red tape for educators. Finally, if performance and growth scores are low, it could be time to revise how educators seek and receive feedback. As we explored in chapter 1 (page 16), normalizing coaching feedback (rather than evaluative feedback) is an excellent micro-move to clarify performance expectations and provide an effective dose of efficacy-enhancing information.

We provide a template and prompts for building well-being profiles in the "Planning for Action to Overcome Uncertainty" reproducible (page 98).

Addressing Teachers' Concerns

We noted earlier the uncertainty about changes in school administration, policies, and programs can cause educators undue stress. When school systems introduce changes, teachers go through predictable stages of concern. This is the premise of researchers Gene E. Hall and Shirley M. Hord's (2015) Concerns Based Adoption Model. Hall and Hord (2015) examined change in schools and identified predictable aspects of change based on their extensive studies. One element of their model, Stages of Concern (SoC), deals with the *affective* dimension of change—that is, teachers' *feelings* and *perceptions* about change. When principals acknowledge and address teachers' feelings and emotions as part of the change process, it can create more positive affective states and therefore can increase their sense of efficacy.

Tapping Into the Sources of Efficacy

Affective states are one of the sources of efficacy-shaping information for individuals and teams (Bandura, 2000). Positive feelings increase efficacy and negative feelings diminish it.

Hall and Hord (2015) identify seven SoCs for principals to be aware of when supporting teachers through change. Let's consider the first four stages.

1. **Unconcerned:** This stage usually happens early on—before teachers realize the required change is going to impact them personally.
2. **Informational:** At the next stage, teachers are seeking information. They want to know what exactly the new initiative entails.
3. **Personal:** At this stage, teachers have personal concerns. For example, they might be concerned about how much of their time learning the new initiative will take and what they need to do to prepare. They are uncertain about the demands required and concerned about how the change will impact them personally.
4. **Management:** The next stage is management concerns. At this stage, teachers are concerned about managing the new initiative as part of their daily routine.

Hall and Hord (2006) refer to these first four SoCs as "self and task" concerns. Their research demonstrates that most change processes begin with almost everyone "having more intense informational and personal concerns from the very beginning" (p. 141). They point out that an often-overlooked aspect is failure to address informational concerns early on. When teachers don't know what's happening, it is perfectly normal for personal concerns to become more intense. In other words, the less information they have, the higher teachers' personal concerns will be. Hall and Hord (2006, 2015) also observe that teachers' personal concerns are often related to uncertainty about expectations and self-doubts about their ability to succeed with the new way (that is, a lack of efficacy).

Once teachers' self and task concerns are alleviated and they have gained clarity about managing the change in their daily practice, their concerns shift to impact. The three impact-related SoCs are as follows.

5. **Consequence:** Teachers with consequence-related concerns want to know how the new initiative will affect their students. "How will my students benefit from this? How can I make this most beneficial for my students?"
6. **Collaboration:** Teachers with collaboration-related concerns have questions about helping their colleagues. They want to know how they can share their knowledge and insights about what they have learned so their colleagues might benefit.
7. **Refocusing:** Teachers with refocusing-related concerns are mainly concerned about finding ways to make the new initiative even more effective. This is the stage where teachers have become so comfortable with the change that they own it and are interested in finding ways to make it even more impactful.

The Stages of Concern model is based on the premise that "the best way to facilitate change utilizes strategies that are aligned with the concerns of those who are engaged with the change" (Hall & Hord, 2006, p. 138). Principals can get a sense of teachers' concerns so they can address them at the appropriate SoC and reduce the effect that uncertainty can have on efficacy. For example, Hall and Hord (2015) suggest that for teachers experiencing personal concerns, it's best to legitimize the existence and expression of these concerns. School leaders can provide encouragement while reinforcing teachers' competence and capability. Principals can connect teachers with others whose personal concerns have diminished and who will be supportive and provide greater clarity. Providing vicarious opportunities for teachers to learn about how their colleagues are overcoming barriers and meeting with success helps to build their efficacy.

Principals can help teachers effectively cope with the changes by listening to teachers' concerns and aligning support with teachers' specific SoC. Keep in mind that teachers with intense informational concerns don't want to hear about philosophy. Teachers with intense personal concerns don't want to hear about innovation. They need clarity on how changes are going to impact them personally. By listening to determine teachers' current SoC, principals can more effectively support them through change, create greater clarity, and foster a greater sense of well-being.

Vicarious experiences are one of the sources of efficacy (Bandura, 2000).

Increasing Interpersonal Clarity

The final micro-move for prioritizing wellness is to increase interpersonal clarity. As noted earlier, when we try to make sense of other people's behavior, we almost always make up a story about it and these narratives are often more unfavorable than the reality (Bushe, 2010). Negative stories then become the input for further episodes of sense making. *Sense making* is the process by which individuals give meaning to their and other people's experiences, especially when confronted with new, complex, or ambiguous situations. Sense making can help teachers navigate uncertainty and adapt to change. However, cognitive biases and emotions that may lead to misinterpretations (that is, interpersonal mush) and faulty assumptions can also influence sense making.

Bushe (2010) describes interpersonal mush as the core of a dysfunctional organization. He finds that people don't ask each other directly what is going on, so a lot of energy goes into sense making. Bushe (2010) writes, "No matter how excited or hopeful we were when we started the partnership, unless we regularly clear out the mush, it grows and becomes more and more toxic until the partnership falls apart" (p. 35). Since people are not going to stop trying to make sense out of one another's experiences, it's helpful for principals to acknowledge these processes and make them visible. By doing so, school leaders clear away the interpersonal mush and prioritize well-being. Bushe (2010) notes, "no matter what is getting in the way of collaborative work relationships, there is one solution that almost always makes it better: increase interpersonal clarity" (p. 43).

Research demonstrates that people vary in their ability to tolerate uncertainty and often, people try to control or eliminate it as much as they can (Laposa et al., 2022). Psychologists call these reactions "intolerance of uncertainty." Being intolerant of uncertainty can cause problems because people tend to invent untested theories to help them make sense of other people's decisions and behavior.

Tapping Into the Sources of Efficacy

Increasing interpersonal clarity in a school can foster positive affective states by reducing misunderstandings and faulty assumptions that arise when people try to make sense of others' behaviors. Principals can model and encourage being more descriptive about one's own thoughts, feelings, and desires, as well as being genuinely curious and nonjudgmental in seeking to understand others' perspectives and experiences.

Principals can increase interpersonal clarity in schools in two ways: by being more descriptive and being more curious. To ensure that teachers have greater clarity about what leaders are experiencing, it's important for principals to be very descriptive about what they are thinking, feeling, and wanting. By doing so, there will be greater accuracy in the stories teachers create as they engage in sense making. Modeling curiosity about other people's experiences is a strategy that will help clear up interpersonal mush as well. This means approaching others with genuine interest and openness, and seeking to understand their perspectives and experiences without judgment. For example, principals could ask, "Can you tell me more about what happened from your perspective?" or "What was that experience like for you?" By being genuinely curious, principals create space for educators to share their experiences and for everyone to develop more accurate understandings of people's reality.

Collective Impact

When school leaders successfully prioritize well-being and overcome the detrimental effects of uncertainty, they create an environment where collective efficacy can flourish. By building workplace well-being profiles, addressing teachers' concerns, and increasing interpersonal clarity, principals can foster a culture of trust, adaptability, and continuous growth. School leaders have the power to create a sense of stability and purpose amid the inevitable changes and challenges that arise in education. By actively listening to teachers' concerns, providing timely and relevant information, and demonstrating genuine curiosity about their experiences, effective efficacy builders cultivate a sense of psychological safety for teacher teams to navigate uncertainty with confidence and resilience. The path to collective impact is paved with a commitment to well-being—it is the foundation on which teachers can embrace change, innovate in their practice, and work together to achieve extraordinary results for their students. When school leaders prioritize wellness, schools become places where uncertainty is met with optimism and a shared belief in the power of collective efficacy to drive transformative change for all learners.

Uncertainty is an enemy of efficacy because it evokes a wide array of emotional phenomena (Morriss et al., 2023). Synonyms for the word *uncertainty* include *anxiety, concern, distrust, doubt, suspicion, uneasiness*, and *worry*. Unfortunately, due to the nature of our working environment, and despite the best-laid plans, feelings of uncertainty are sometimes unavoidable. However, effective efficacy builders can overcome uncertainty through a focus on well-being. Micro-moves to promote positive workplace well-being in this chapter include creating workplace well-being profiles, taking steps to address teachers' concerns, and increasing interpersonal clarity. Use the exercises and prompts in the reproducible "Planning for Action to Overcome Uncertainty" (page 98) to practice prioritizing teachers' well-being.

Planning for Action to Overcome Uncertainty

Use the following exercises and prompts to engage with the micro-moves discussed in chapter 6.

Workplace Well-Being Profiles

Adapted from Amy Green's (2022) model of workplace well-being, the following reflective prompts show how workplace well-being and collective efficacy help teachers navigate uncertainty. Have teachers complete the following profile. For each point, ask teachers to evaluate themselves on a scale from 1 (lowest) to 5 (highest).

Workplace Well-Being Priority	Reflective Prompts
Engagement	I enjoy working with my team. ○ 1 ○ 2 ○ 3 ○ 4 ○ 5 The work I do makes a difference. ○ 1 ○ 2 ○ 3 ○ 4 ○ 5 My contributions are valued and recognized. ○ 1 ○ 2 ○ 3 ○ 4 ○ 5 I have positive and collaborative relationships with others. ○ 1 ○ 2 ○ 3 ○ 4 ○ 5 If I feel low levels of engagement, I know how to shift to higher levels of engagement. ○ 1 ○ 2 ○ 3 ○ 4 ○ 5
Productivity	I am clear on our school priorities and how I contribute. ○ 1 ○ 2 ○ 3 ○ 4 ○ 5 I can effectively and efficiently prioritize tasks and workload. ○ 1 ○ 2 ○ 3 ○ 4 ○ 5

Productivity (cont.)	I accomplish tasks in a timely manner and know what's required. ○ 1 ○ 2 ○ 3 ○ 4 ○ 5 I actively seek out new ways to do things to be effective and efficient. ○ 1 ○ 2 ○ 3 ○ 4 ○ 5 If I feel low levels of productivity, I reflect, restrategize, and change. ○ 1 ○ 2 ○ 3 ○ 4 ○ 5
Performance and Growth	The strategies I implement are having an impact. ○ 1 ○ 2 ○ 3 ○ 4 ○ 5 I set professional goals and seek feedback and support. ○ 1 ○ 2 ○ 3 ○ 4 ○ 5 I have a growth mindset and am open to and regularly seek out professional learning to improve. ○ 1 ○ 2 ○ 3 ○ 4 ○ 5 I gather feedback from my students, colleagues, and school leaders. ○ 1 ○ 2 ○ 3 ○ 4 ○ 5 If I didn't perform as well as I would like, I reflect and know where to seek help or adjust my strategy. ○ 1 ○ 2 ○ 3 ○ 4 ○ 5

After teachers complete the profile, facilitate a team meeting and work through a process for each team member to share their well-being profile. Within a culture of trust and respect, demonstrate openness and vulnerability to discuss the scores. Openly share ideas for improvement.

Finally, as a team, set a collective goal with an accompanying strategy to move the workplace well-being scores forward.

Addressing Teachers' Concerns

Gene E. Hall and Shirley M. Hord's (2015) Stages of Concern, outlined in the following chart, may be used as a graphic organizer during a change process. List the proposed change at the top and brainstorm as a team using the reflective questions for each stage.

Stage of Concern	Proposed Change: ____________________ (For example, the introduction of a new mathematics curriculum)
Unconcerned	Although educators are unconcerned at this stage, leaders could ready themselves for the upcoming Stages of Concern.
Informational	What do educators need to know to enact this change? What key information will they need?
Personal	How might this change personally impact educators? Are there strong personal objections to the change?
Management	How will this change impact daily routines? What time will be required? Will training need to take place?
Consequence	How will the new initiative affect students? How will students benefit from this? How can this be most beneficial for students?
Collaboration	How can I help my colleagues through this change? How can we connect and collaborate?
Refocusing	What has been the impact of the change? What could we do to refocus our efforts? Where can we improve?

Increasing Interpersonal Clarity

Think about a recent situation where you or someone else in the school may have made assumptions about another person's behavior or intentions. Consider how being more descriptive or curious could have led to a better understanding and outcome. Record your thoughts in the space below.

List three to five ways you can be more descriptive about your own thoughts, feelings, and desires when communicating with teachers and staff.

List three to five ways you can model and encourage curiosity and nonjudgmental listening when seeking to understand others' perspectives and experiences.

Choose one strategy for being more descriptive and one for being more curious that you will implement in the coming week. For example, you could use a template to increase interpersonal clarity by outlining what people might see, hear, and feel in the situation you've chosen. Another strategy may be to capture teachers' wonderings or worries. Capturing key questions will give you insight into areas where you need to be more clear.

Next, choose one strategy to trial, write down your commitment to test out the strategy, and set a calendar reminder to follow through on your actions.

After implementing the strategies, reflect on their impact and effectiveness. Seek feedback from others on how well you communicated and listened. Adjust your approach as needed and continue practicing so increasing interpersonal clarity becomes a habit.

Reference

Green, A. (2022). Teacher wellbeing: A real conversation for teachers and leaders. *Melbourne, Victoria, Australia: Amba Press.*

Hall, G. E., & Hord, S. M. (2015). Implementing change: Patterns, principles, and potholes *(4th ed.). Boston: Pearson.*

Part 3

Mastery Experiences

Mastery experiences are the most potent source of collective efficacy as they provide authentic evidence that the team has what it takes to succeed. As we defined the term earlier, *mastery experiences* are collaborative success on a challenging task, and Bandura (1998) writes that "the most effective way of instilling a strong sense of efficacy is through mastery experiences" (p. 53). Experiencing success builds a robust sense of belief that further success is possible, while failure undermines efficacy, particularly if the failure occurs before efficacy levels can be firmly established. A word of caution, however: if success comes too easily, educators aren't challenged and can come to expect quick results. When resistance does eventually come, teams can quickly become discouraged by failure. Therefore, mastery experiences are most effective when there's been a sense of challenge. Bandura (1997) writes that "a resilient sense of efficacy requires experience in overcoming obstacles through persevering effort" (p. 80).

Failure isn't necessarily fatal to collective efficacy, though. Principals who encounter difficulties and setbacks in their pursuits can use these barriers to reinforce that success requires a well-executed strategy, persistence, and sustained effort. Difficult situations provide opportunities to learn how to regroup, restrategize, and turn failed efforts into future success. When school teams become convinced that they have what it takes to succeed, they overcome the hurdles in front of them, persist despite the setbacks, and bounce back from failed attempts. Principals who can create this type of efficacious culture develop school teams that are stronger and more able in times of adversity.

Schools build to high levels of collective efficacy through mastery moments. These are the defining moments for educators that shape our experiences and influence our levels of efficacy. Authors Chip Heath and Dan Heath (2017) describe mastery moments as moments that rise above the everyday, rewire our understanding of ourselves or the world, capture us at our best, and are social. Mastery moments are experiences that are memorable and meaningful and shape the beliefs of teachers. They are the instances in which educators experience success and attribute their success to their efforts, strategy, or actions.

We have witnessed firsthand that powerful collaborative experiences serve as defining moments that significantly strengthen collective efficacy. One specific example took place in a school district in Ontario, Canada, where teams of teachers set the goal to improve students' nonfiction writing. During the course of the project, teachers engaged in a cyclical, iterative process that involved gathering evidence of student learning, clarifying a focus area, identifying goals and learning needs, trying and testing specific evidence-based strategies in classrooms, collaboratively analyzing student work, and evaluating the impact of these changes on student achievement.

Through this process, teachers were able to identify areas of improvement and respond accordingly. For example, when teachers determined from their assessment that some students provided insufficient supporting details for a topic, teachers used a set of worked examples that ranged in proficiency (for example, little or no supporting details to many connected and relevant supporting details) with students to help them self-assess their own writing compared to the worked examples. Once students identified "How am I doing?," teachers gave additional support through instruction and feedback, such as modeling how to add supporting details including examples, statistics, analogies, or explanations.

Results demonstrated that more than 80 percent of the marker students made significant gains in achievement. The results proved not only confirming to teachers but also eye opening as they realized how their efforts resulted in measurable increases for the students in their classrooms. Educators saw themselves as agents of influence (Donohoo, Bryen, & Weishar, 2018). When teams recognized small successes early on and attributed student progress to factors that were within their realm of influence (for example, actions of the team and individual teachers' changes in practice), they were motivated to continue. The recognition of mastery experiences unfolded as teachers shared their learning and successes with their peers.

Principals cannot rely on these experiences to just happen; they might come sporadically, be ad hoc, or be inaccessible to the staff who need them. Principals need to be cognizant that defining moments can be consciously created. School leaders can be architects of moments that matter. Principals can structure situations for teachers in ways that bring about success and avoid placing them prematurely in situations where they are unlikely to succeed.

In the three chapters in part 3, we identify three enemies of efficacy and offer micro-moves designed to provide the conditions in which leaders can create mastery experiences. Key aspects include shaping the conditions for educators to take action and tackle challenges head-on rather than avoiding them, determining what success looks like by designing the requirements for positive outcomes, and empowering teachers through teacher leadership. By shaping environments that are conducive to experiencing mastery moments, principals can enhance collective teacher efficacy. A principal can effectively orchestrate mastery moments by embedding reflection into teachers' daily routines, helping teachers measure progress against a predetermined criterion, and developing teachers as leaders.

In part 3, we discuss the following micro-moves.

- By *posing reflective questions*, principals can encourage teachers to think critically, reflect deeply, and engage in substantive professional dialogue, all of which leads to ongoing learning, growth, and improvement in their practice.
- By *modeling evidence-based reflection*, principals reinforce the message that reflection is a valued and expected practice.
- By *guiding strengths-based approaches*, principals enhance teachers' feelings of competence and self-worth and evoke positive emotions such as pride and joy.
- *Setting mastery goals* can trigger intrinsic motivation, which is valuable in stimulating individual and collective action.
- *Identifying criterion-based success* based on a predetermined criterion provides educators with a means to gauge progress toward mastery goals.
- By *providing goal-referenced feedback*, principals provide information about progress toward goals, recognize achievements made by the team, and offer guidance for improvement.
- By *validating informal leadership*, principals strengthen teachers' capacity to lead.
- By *expanding opportunities for formal leadership*, principals create cultures of innovation and risk taking.
- By *increasing teacher autonomy and decision-making power*, principals let teachers know their opinions are valued, which makes teachers more likely to feel invested in the outcomes and committed to the success of new initiatives.

Chapter 7

Action Over Avoidance

By *embedding reflection into teachers' daily routines*, school leaders can overcome *avoidance* as an enemy of efficacy.

In this chapter, we examine how avoidance becomes an enemy of efficacy. School leaders can overcome avoidance by making reflection a routine part of teachers' practice. Three key micro-moves leaders can rely on include posing reflective questions, modeling evidence-based reflection, and guiding strengths-based approaches. School leaders achieve collective impact as they overcome judgment by making self-reflection routine for teachers.

Avoidance as an Enemy of Efficacy

Avoidance is a coping mechanism, and it can be a good thing when people are confronted with risky or dangerous situations. Avoidance becomes problematic, however, when educators avoid the things that can help them grow and get better—and ultimately help their students grow and get better. It's natural for teachers to want to avoid things that make them uncomfortable, such as the following.

- Opening up their classroom doors and making their teaching more public
- Engaging in conversations about race and discrimination
- Examining their own biases and assumptions
- Challenging the status quo and advocating for improvements

Engaging with that discomfort, however, is a crucial aspect of their professional and personal development.

When teachers avoid collaborative endeavors that might cause them to step outside their comfort zone, they are missing out on opportunities to learn from and with one another. Furthermore, by avoiding uncomfortable conversations, especially when they are related to issues of bias and inequity, educators may inadvertently maintain the status quo. Therefore, avoidance is an enemy of efficacy. Consider the following three hypothetical examples of avoidance.

1. The principal at Northville High School had recently announced a new initiative encouraging teachers to share exemplary student work with their colleagues to promote evidence-based practices and celebrate student achievement. Mrs. Jones, an experienced English teacher, felt a sense of unease as she finished grading her student essays. She knew that sharing student work was a good idea, but the thought of others reviewing her students' writing made her stomach churn. Despite her years of experience and dedication to teaching, Mrs. Jones couldn't shake the feeling that her students' work might not measure up to the high standards set by her colleagues. She made the decision to miss the next collaborative team meeting because she wanted to avoid bringing her students' writing for others to examine.
2. Mr. Greene, a middle school mathematics teacher known for working independently, had been teaching for over a decade. He believed that planning with other teachers would only slow him down and compromise his autonomy. Whenever the principal promoted teacher collaboration, Mr. Greene would retreat to his own classroom. Mid-way through the year, the mathematics coach suggested that teachers work together to create interdisciplinary units. Mr. Greene quietly rolled his eyes and replied that he had no interest in sharing his ideas or working with others. He was convinced that his way was the best and most efficient way and therefore avoided working with his colleagues.
3. The new principal at West Gate School felt that she had her work cut out for her. She noticed that the teachers responsible for placing incoming English learners held unrecognized biases that influenced their selection of courses for multilingual learners new to the school. In one example, the placement team reviewed student records, including their English proficiency test scores. Despite students showing promise and potential in certain subject areas, the focus was primarily on students' language skills. The mathematics teacher, Mr. Fox, looked at one student's file and commented, "Her English scores are pretty low. I don't think she'll be

> able to keep up in my algebra II class. Let's put her in the basic math course instead." The science teacher, Ms. Anderson, nodded in agreement. "I have the same concern. These students will struggle with the complex vocabulary in biology. It's best to place them in the general science course, where the content is more accessible." There was even an instance where the team placed a senior (twelfth-grade student) in a sophomore (tenth grade) physical education class because of his lack of English proficiency. When asked by their principal to reflect on the potential biases in their placement of English learners, the team avoided acknowledging any biases, minimized the principal's concerns, and attributed it to her being oversensitive.

In the first two examples, teachers avoided opportunities to engage in professional learning or collaborate with their colleagues. When teachers avoid sharing effective teaching strategies and student work, they miss the opportunity to learn from one another's successes and incorporate new ideas into their own classrooms. When teachers avoid collaborating and planning with their colleagues, they miss the opportunity to create more consistent experiences for students across classrooms, give and receive support, and feel less isolated in their work. In the third example, teachers were reluctant to critically examine their own implicit biases. This lack of critical reflection can limit students' opportunities and academic growth. In this respect, avoidance is an enemy of efficacy.

Another way in which avoidance is problematic is when school leaders sweep conflict under the rug or smooth it over. Conflict can make school leaders feel uncomfortable, and avoidance is understandable if they have not learned how to manage disagreements. When conflict is neglected, it does not disappear and can quickly result in damaged relationships, increased stress, and low morale. This is another reason why avoidance is an enemy of efficacy.

Researchers Hagit Inbar-Furst and Thomas P. Gumpel's (2015) study reveals that teachers avoided seeking help from colleagues because of fear of failure and a desire to deal with problems independently.

Peggy A. Ertmer, Anne T. Ottenbreit-Leftwich, Olgun Sadik, Emine Sendurur and Polat Sendurur (2012) find that teachers avoid integrating technology because they lack confidence, knowledge, and skills.

Researchers Britta K. Morris-Rothschild and Marla R. Brassard (2006) find that teachers with high classroom management efficacy and security of attachment (low on avoidance and anxiety) were predicted to endorse positive classroom management strategies more than teachers low in classroom management efficacy. Classroom management efficacy had positive significant effects on use of integrating and compromising strategies, while avoidance had negative effects on both and anxiety on integrating strategies.

To realize systemic and sustainable improvement in schools, principals can create cultures where avoidance is minimized and action is prioritized. The belief that teachers and school leaders can improve educational outcomes for students becomes the foundation for action. Bandura (1998) states that "unless people believe they can produce desired effects by their actions they have little incentive to act. Efficacy belief is, therefore, the foundation of action" (p. 52). Bandura (1997) also suggests that it would be advantageous to equip "people with a firm belief that they can produce valued efforts by their collective action" (p. 477). System and school leaders can take intentional steps to increase collective efficacy and overcome avoidance as an enemy of efficacy.

Overcome Avoidance With Reflection

School principals can overcome avoidance and help educators take greater action on issues that matter most. This begins with having a shared purpose, clear priorities, and consensus on goals. From there, school leaders can help to reduce problematic avoidance behaviors and initiate action by embedding reflection in teachers' daily routines. Reflective teachers are more likely to question the status quo, take risks, and try innovative approaches rather than default to how things have always been done. Reflection is a powerful tool for educators to critically examine their own beliefs, attitudes, and practices, including implicit biases that may influence their interactions with students and their teaching practices. Through reflection, principals can help teachers gain clarity on what they're doing well and see the positive results of their work. By doing so, principals capitalize on mastery experiences to strengthen collective efficacy.

By cultivating a habit of reflection, principals help teachers develop a stronger sense of efficacy, which in turn empowers them to take proactive steps to improve their practice and student learning. Instead of avoiding challenges or feeling overwhelmed, reflective teachers are more likely to embrace a growth mindset, persist in the face of obstacles, and actively seek ways to enhance their effectiveness in the classroom.

Embedding reflection into teachers' daily routines is about teachers working together and examining sources of student evidence that can inform their work (Donohoo, O'Leary, & Hattie, 2020). Donohoo and colleagues (2018) write, "When instructional improvement efforts result in improved student outcomes that are validated through sources of student learning data, educators' collective efficacy is strengthened. Evidence of collective impact, in turn, reinforces proactive collective behaviors, feelings, thoughts, and motivations" (p. 42). Embedded reflection on evidence helps uncover cause-and-effect relationships (quality teaching causes student learning) and would therefore highlight firsthand mastery experiences and vicarious experiences for teacher teams. Teachers come to realize the positive results of their own efforts, others' efforts, and their combined efforts through processes that enable embedded reflective practices.

Scholars Jennifer York-Barr, William A. Sommers, Gail S. Ghere, and Jo Montie (2006) note that when educators engage in reflective practice, efficacy increases as they notice the positive effects of their actions. York-Barr and colleagues (2006) write, "As the internal capacities of teachers to learn and make a positive difference are recognized and harnessed, a collective sense of efficacy and empowerment emerges" (p. 14). This is the essence of a mastery experience.

When teachers regularly reflect on their experiences, analyze student data, and critically examine their instructional strategies, they gain valuable insights into what works and what doesn't in their classrooms. This process of self-assessment and self-awareness helps teachers identify areas for improvement and develop targeted action plans to address challenges. Reflection empowers teachers to take ownership of their professional growth and actively seek solutions to problems they encounter. Instead of avoiding difficult situations, reflective teachers are more likely to proactively explore new approaches, seek support from colleagues, and persist in finding ways to improve student outcomes. The increased sense of efficacy that comes from reflection can motivate teachers to take risks, try innovative strategies, and push through setbacks. Furthermore, when teachers engage in collaborative reflection with peers, they benefit from the collective wisdom and support of their colleagues. Sharing challenges, brainstorming solutions, and learning from each other's successes can further boost teachers' confidence and willingness to tackle difficulties head-on. Three micro-moves for embedding reflection into teachers' daily routines include (1) posing reflective questions, (2) modeling evidence-based reflection, and (3) guiding strengths-based approaches.

Posing Reflective Questions

Principals can hone their questioning skills to facilitate teacher and team reflection. This micro-move involves using questioning strategies to facilitate evidence-based reflective conversations that help teacher teams in moving beyond surface-level discussions and engaging in critical analysis of their practice and its impact on student learning. By modeling reflective questions, principals can help teachers internalize this skill and increase the likelihood that they will pose reflective questions to themselves and each other. Furthermore, by employing this small but impactful micro-move, principals can help turn the ideas and realizations from the reflection into real improvements in what teachers and teacher teams do. In other words, skilled questioning by a principal not only encourages teachers to reflect deeply on their practice but also helps them take the crucial next step of transforming those reflective insights into concrete actions that positively impact their teaching and their students' learning.

Reflective questions are open-ended questions. This type of question allows for a wide range of answers and encourages deeper thinking and discussion. Unlike closed questions that can be answered with a simple *yes* or *no* or a brief, factual response to open-ended questions invite the teacher or team to share their opinions and insights in a more detailed and expansive way. They often start with words like *what*, *how*, *why*, or *in what ways*, and they encourage teachers to provide more than just a one-word or short-phrase answer. For example: "How did the new instructional strategy impact student engagement and learning, and what insights did you gain from implementing it?" as opposed to "Did the new instructional strategy work well?"

Finally, when posing reflective questions, it's important to invite participation from all team members and ensure that everyone has the opportunity to contribute their insights and ideas. Principals can pay attention to patterns of participation and directly invite quieter teachers to share or gently redirect dominant voices to ensure a balance of perspectives. By acknowledging and validating each team member's contributions, principals can use them as springboards for further discussion, demonstrating that everyone's perspective is valued.

Tapping Into the Sources of Efficacy

Principals' use of reflective questioning to guide teacher teams in evidence-based discussions and action planning can directly contribute to mastery experiences, which in turn serve as a powerful source of collective teacher efficacy.

Consider the following open-ended reflective questions principals can use for various purposes depending on their need, context, and the situation.

- Questions about evidence
    - What evidence from student work supports your observations?
    - How might we collect data to test our hypotheses?
    - As you reflect on the evidence or examples you've shared, what patterns, trends, or underlying factors do you notice?
    - What specific student behaviors or learning outcomes have you observed that led you to this conclusion?
    - As we examine these data, what questions arise that we haven't yet explored, and what additional evidence might we need to deepen our inquiry and inform our next steps?
- Questions that link outcomes with effort
    - Based on these successes, what have you learned about your collective ability to impact student learning and how can we build on these strengths moving forward?
    - What are the key factors in our team's ability to support students and how can we apply these lessons to ensure ongoing progress?
    - What insights can we gain about our collective ability to create inclusive and supportive learning environments?
- Questions that foster perspective taking
    - What personal experiences or cultural backgrounds might influence our perceptions of student behavior or learning?
    - How might this situation look different from the student's or family's point of view?
    - What cultural factors might impact students' experiences or reactions?
    - What assumptions might we be making about this student or group of students based on their background?
    - How might our instructional strategies privilege certain learning styles or cultural norms?
- Questions that probe for deeper understanding
    - What makes you say that?
    - Can you provide a specific example to illustrate your point?

    - What experiences or observations have led you to that conclusion?
    - Can you walk me through your thought process on this issue and share any evidence or examples that have shaped your current understanding?
    - What insights are emerging that might not have been apparent at first glance?
- Questions that prompt action
    - How might this evidence inform your future instructional decisions?
    - Based on our discussion, what might be some next steps for improving student learning?
    - Given the insights we've gained, what are our next steps?
    - As we look ahead to the next school year, what are some areas of professional growth you'd like to focus on?
    - What action steps can we take to support each other in achieving our goals?
- Questions for conceptual understanding
    - What is the relationship between teacher collaboration and student achievement?
    - What is the relationship between teacher self-reflection and professional growth?
    - How do the principles of trust, vulnerability, and shared responsibility shape the dynamics of effective teacher collaboration?
    - What is the relationship between teacher agency, autonomy, and collaboration?
    - What is the relationship between collective teacher efficacy and student achievement?

By devising questions that engage teacher teams in deep reflection, principals help teachers identify gaps in student learning, ineffective instructional practices, or other areas for improvement that may not be immediately apparent. Reflective questions can also help teacher teams identify and reflect on their own internal biases by promoting self-awareness, empathy, and cultural responsiveness.

Modeling Evidence-Based Reflection

Another micro-move for embedding evidence-based reflection into teachers' daily routines is to model it. During discussions, faculty meetings, or collaborative team meetings, principals can model the process of reflecting on schoolwide evidence and how it informs decision making. This helps set the expectation that reflection should be based on evidence rather than assumptions.

After presenting data, principals model the process of reflecting on what the data suggest about the school's strengths, areas for growth, and potential next steps. Principals can use a think-aloud strategy, posing questions like, "What do these data tell us about the effectiveness of our current practices? What are we doing well that we should continue or expand? What areas do we need to focus on improving?" Principals can make connections between the data and school goals and initiatives by modeling how to use data to monitor progress and evaluate the effectiveness of different strategies.

Principals can also share examples of decisions based on reflection and data analysis. One example comes from a school in Minneapolis–Saint Paul. After noticing that chronic absenteeism rates had been increasing, the leadership team sat down and disaggregated attendance records by grade level, student demographics, and time of year. They noticed that absenteeism rates were the highest among ninth-grade students, that students from low-income families were more likely to be chronically absent, and that attendance dipped significantly during the winter months. The leadership team reached out to teachers to brainstorm strategies to address this issue.

In a faculty meeting, the principal explained how the attendance data prompted a new approach to family outreach. He shared the process with the entire faculty by presenting the initial attendance data that sparked the inquiry and walking teachers through the process of how they disaggregated and analyzed the evidence. He then explained how the data analysis led to specific and targeted interventions, outlining the strategies the team chose to implement as a result.

As the school implemented the attendance strategies, the principal continued to model evidence-based reflection by regularly reviewing updated attendance data with teachers. Together, they collaboratively assessed whether the interventions were working, identified challenges that emerged, and made adjustments as needed. By consistently sharing and reflecting on real examples like this, the principal demonstrated the value and impact of using data to guide improvement efforts. Over time, this helped create a schoolwide culture where staff regularly and effectively used data to inform practice at all levels, from individual classroom decisions to schoolwide initiatives.

Guiding Strengths-Based Approaches

Embedded reflective practices are a key enabling condition to build collective efficacy (Arzonetti Hite & Donohoo, 2021). Reflective practices produce efficacy as teams process information together, reflect on progress, determine next steps, and attribute success to their actions. However, reflection isn't always positive. Some teams of teachers become so self-critical it impacts their team function and well-being. Teachers are often their harshest critics as they critique their own performance, ultimately building a sense of guilt or a feeling they haven't done enough. When teachers view themselves in this deficit way, uncertainty creeps in and can impact collective efficacy. Stefani Arzonetti Hite and Jenni Donohoo (2021) write, "When teams of teachers engage in reflective practices, it helps to uncover beliefs and assumptions that drive actions and shift causal attributions for success and/or failure" (p. 79).

A simple micro-move for leaders is to begin flipping educators' mindset when reflecting on their progress. Typically, reflective practices begin by examining a problem of practice or something that isn't working as well as intended. Collective efficacy is built from success, and this flipped approach focuses on strengths rather than deficits or problems.

Strengths-based approaches involve focusing on one's strengths, talents, and positive qualities rather than dwelling on weaknesses or shortcomings. Some simple methods for strengths-based reflection include the following.

- **Identifying strengths:** Reflect on past experiences and identify moments where you felt confident, successful, or accomplished. Pay attention to activities or tasks that energized you and consider what strengths were at play.
- **Reflective journaling:** Keep a journal where you regularly write about moments when you felt strong, capable, and fulfilled. Reflect on the skills and qualities that contributed to those experiences.
- **Goal setting with strengths in mind:** When setting goals, align them with your strengths. Consider how you can leverage your strengths to achieve your objectives more effectively.
- **Strengths-based peer support groups:** Join a team where members discuss and leverage their strengths. Engaging with others who share similar values can provide support and inspiration.

Tapping Into the Sources of Efficacy

Guiding strengths-based approaches can lead to mastery experiences for teachers. By focusing on their strengths and positive qualities during reflection rather than dwelling on weaknesses or problems, teachers can build confidence, resilience, and a sense of accomplishment, which all contribute to their collective efficacy.

By incorporating these simple methods into team routines, principals can cultivate a strengths-based mindset that enhances self-awareness, increases resilience, and positively influences well-being in their schools.

Let's look at an example of this in practice. A primary school principal in Brisbane, Queensland, Australia, uses learning cycle triads as a strengths-based approach to improve outcomes. In this collaborative, short-term data-cycle practice, triads of teachers routinely celebrate practices that *have* improved student progress. From there, teachers inquire together about how they can build on the practices that led to success. Teachers also consider how they can transfer these practices to encourage more students to set strengths-based goals. The second phase of this process occurs five weeks later, when the triad reflects together and shares successes they achieved with the strategy enacted from the previous triad meeting. During these strengths-focused meetings, teachers communicate their incremental gains even when they haven't achieved their targeted goals.

By reflecting on strengths, this process increases teacher confidence in sharing, celebrating the small gains, and improving positivity when determining the next progression for student learning.

Collective Impact

When school leaders successfully embed reflection into teachers' daily routines and overcome the detrimental effects of avoidance, they create an environment where collective efficacy can thrive. By posing reflective questions, modeling evidence-based reflection, and guiding strengths-based approaches, principals can foster a culture of continuous learning, innovation, and growth. School leaders can create opportunities for teachers to engage in meaningful reflection, share their successes and challenges, and learn from one another. By modeling evidence-based reflection, principals create a culture where teachers habitually use data to inform their own reflections and decisions rather than rely on assumptions or anecdotal evidence alone. Collective impact results from a commitment to action—it is the foundation on which teachers can overcome their discomfort, take risks, and work together to achieve extraordinary results for their students. By embedding reflection into teachers' daily routines, school leaders create environments where avoidance is replaced by a shared sense of purpose, a willingness to experiment, and a focus on leveraging individual and collective strengths to drive transformative change for all learners. Collective impact is achieved when highly efficacious teams take action.

Avoidance is an enemy of efficacy because people tend to avoid the things that make them uncomfortable and engaging with discomfort is a critical aspect of professional growth. An effective efficacy builder can overcome avoidance by embedding reflection into teachers' daily routines. Embedded reflective practices are at the heart of teachers' collaborative work. When teachers reflect on student evidence in their common practices and see results because of that reflection, it spurs further action. The micro-moves in this chapter include enabling connection and collaboration, encouraging experimentation, and guiding strengths-based approaches.

On a final note, while this chapter was mostly about teachers avoiding things, it's important for school leaders to recognize their own avoidance tendencies and model positive behaviors. Use the exercises and prompts in the reproducible "Planning for Action to Overcome Avoidance" (page 119) to practice cultivating teacher self-reflection.

Planning for Action to Overcome Avoidance

Use the following exercises to engage with the micro-moves discussed in chapter 7.

Posing Reflective Questions

Identify scenarios related to student learning and teacher practice (for example, a grade-level team has noticed a pattern of students struggling with problem solving in mathematics) that are currently relevant in your context.

Record two to three reflective questions you could ask a teacher team to facilitate an evidence-based discussion and guide action planning around each scenario.

Review the questions and consider the following:

- How do the questions promote reflection on evidence of student learning?
- How do the questions encourage teachers to link their efforts to student outcomes?
- How might these questions guide the team in developing action steps?

Modeling Evidence-Based Reflection

Determine specific evidence that you would like teachers to reflect on (for example, student engagement levels, classroom management strategies, or suspension rates).

Examine the evidence while being aware of your thoughts, ideas, and questions.

Script a think-aloud that you could use to model reflection based on this evidence.

Guiding Strengths-Based Approaches

Reflect on a time where you (or your team) worked through a period of uncertainty. Identify and describe the positive aspects (that is, the things that went well). Describe the strengths you demonstrated through this process and what you learned about yourself, the challenges you may have overcome, and how you've grown.

Chapter 8

Criteria Over Comparison

By *measuring progress against a predetermined criterion*, school leaders can overcome *comparison* as an enemy of efficacy.

In this chapter, we explore how comparison becomes an enemy of efficacy. School leaders can overcome comparison by measuring progress against a predetermined criterion. Three key micro-moves leaders can use include setting mastery goals, identifying criterion-based success, and providing goal-referenced feedback. School leaders achieve collective impact as they help teachers focus on their progress rather than compare themselves to others.

Comparison as an Enemy of Efficacy

Social comparison theory is the idea that success is based on how individuals stack up against others. The theory was first proposed in 1954 by psychologist Leon Festinger, who suggested that people have an innate drive to evaluate themselves, often in comparison to others. Albert Bandura and Forest J. Jourden (1991) note that "social comparative influences affect self-regulatory factors governing human motivation and performance accomplishments" (p. 948). In an experimental study, those who experienced a decline in performance, in comparison to their peers, also exhibited more erratic thinking, self-criticism, and a decrease in self-efficacy (Bandura & Jourden, 1991). Under these conditions, comparison is an enemy of efficacy.

Two preservice teachers, Raquel and Anne Marie, were placed in a grade 7 class in a middle school. As part of their teaching credential requirements, they had to practice teaching for six weeks under the supervision of an experienced teacher. Raquel had an instant rapport with the students, but Anne Marie seemed a bit awkward. Raquel joked with the students and continued to foster relationships over the course of the placement. It was obvious that the students really liked Raquel. Anne Marie was not as successful in creating bonds with the students and over time, her efficacy began to wane.

As she watched Raquel, who seemed so natural at it, Anne Marie started to second guess whether she was cut out for teaching. With each passing day, she took on more of a defeatist attitude. In her mind, it was clear that she couldn't compete with Raquel. When collaborating with Raquel and the supervising teacher, Anne Marie was very self-conscious and held back on sharing her ideas in fear of them being rejected. Although they both were successful in obtaining their teaching certification, Anne Marie's self-efficacy continued to be at risk.

Tapping Into the Sources of Efficacy

"Successes build a robust sense of efficacy. Failures undermine it, especially if failures occur before a sense of efficacy is firmly established" (Bandura, 1998, p. 53).

In a study investigating sources of preservice teachers' self-efficacy, researchers Christopher Niel Prilop, Kira Elena Weber, Frans J. Prins, and Marc Kleinknecht (2021) demonstrate that social comparison plays a factor in self-efficacy beliefs.

A number of research studies have demonstrated a significant and positive relationship between self-efficacy and collective efficacy (Gibbs & Powell, 2012; Goddard & Goddard, 2001; Kurz & Knight, 2004).

Although social comparison theory was initially based on self-comparisons, social comparisons also occur between groups. Professor of social psychology Michael A. Hogg (2000) states, "from these comparisons emerge group norms, group structure, and intergroup relations, which in turn provide the framework for group-based social comparisons" (401). Hogg (2000) also points out that any theory of social groups "would be a strange theory indeed if it did not deal with social comparison processes" (p. 401).

There are both benefits and drawbacks to social comparison. When comparisons motivate teachers and teams to improve, and in the process, they develop a better image of themselves, comparisons can be beneficial. For example, when a school has exceeded expectations and received recognition for their work together, social comparison can be advantageous for collective efficacy. When social comparison is left to take its natural course, however, "the evidence suggests that people are likely to compare in counterproductive ways" (Waltré, Dietz, & Van Knippenberg, 2023,

p. 1). It can promote judgment, negativity, and avoidance—all enemies of efficacy.

To realize systemic and sustainable improvement in schools, principals can reduce the negative aspects of comparison. The drive to compare, in combination with the tendency to compare in counterproductive ways, stresses the need to minimize the drawbacks to social comparison. Leaders can orchestrate mastery experiences by helping teachers measure progress against a predetermined criterion. Such environments, where comparison is minimized, foster learning and growth. System and school leaders can take intentional steps to overcome social comparison as an enemy of efficacy.

Sung-il Kim, Myung-Jin Lee, Yoonkyung Chung, and Mimi Bong's conducted a study in 2010 examining how different types of feedback affect brain activation. They found that norm-referenced feedback (comparing performance to others) activated brain areas associated with negative emotions, while criterion-referenced feedback (based on set standards) did not.

Overcome Comparison With Criteria

School principals can overcome social comparison as an enemy of efficacy by helping teachers measure progress against a predetermined criteria. *Criteria* refer to standards for judgment or decision making. Coupled with goal setting and the right kind of feedback, identifying criteria-based successes can be a powerful way to foster efficacy. After setting goals and determining success criteria, measuring progress will guide the team toward its goals. Furthermore, teachers and teams can then use feedback to make timely adjustments to improvement strategies as needed.

There are two important distinctions to note when measuring success against predetermined criteria. The first is the difference between criterion-referenced and norm-referenced measures. *Criterion-referenced measures* draw comparisons between an individual or team's performance and a predetermined standard. *Norm-referenced measures* draw comparisons between an individual or team's performance and their peers. While the latter are informative and serve a distinct purpose in school-improvement efforts, they can have both positive and negative effects on efficacy depending on how they are interpreted. We are not suggesting that leaders ignore norm-referenced information; however, our focus in this chapter is on criterion-referenced measures.

Studies demonstrate that norm-referenced feedback undermines learners' intrinsic motivation by lowering their interest in the task and preventing them from enjoying learning for the sake of learning (Butler, 1987).

The second important distinction is between two types of goal orientations: mastery and performance. *Mastery-oriented learners* are typically associated with more desirable outcomes such as effort, high engagement, intrinsic motivation, and persistence. In contrast, *performance-oriented learners* tend to focus on demonstrating their abilities relative to others, often prioritizing grades or recognition over deep understanding. We are not suggesting that leaders abandon performance goals. In fact, a combination of mastery and performance goals may be ideal for learning and achievement. However, for the purpose of this chapter, we focus on mastery-oriented goal setting.

Unlike the micro-moves we presented in previous chapters, which can stand on their own, we suggest that you use the moves in this chapter in tandem and iteratively. The three micro-moves for measuring progress against predetermined criteria include (1) setting mastery goals, (2) identifying criteria-based successes, and (3) providing goal-referenced feedback.

According to Hattie's (2023) Visible Learning synthesis, clear goal intentions have an effect size of 0.44.

In a study examining the outcomes of performance goals versus mastery goals, researchers Gerard Seijts and Gary P. Latham (2005) find that when the mastery goal is met, the performance goal takes care of itself.

Setting Mastery Goals

Goals are a desired result that the team envisions, plans, and commits to achieving. As noted earlier, mastery goals trigger intrinsic motivation and can be valuable in stimulating individual and collective action. Goals can be either individual or team level. The following are some examples of individual and interdependent mastery goals set by teachers and teacher teams.

- Our goal is to improve students' ability to develop, select, and apply better problem-solving strategies.
- My goal is to develop stronger classroom management skills so that my students experience a safe, positive, and productive learning environment.
- Our goal is to increase students' desire to read so that they expand their knowledge, vocabulary, imagination, and academic success.

Tapping Into the Sources of Efficacy

Mastery is the number one source of efficacy-shaping information (Bandura, 2000).

Leaders can use the following guidelines to help teachers set mastery goals.

- **Focus on progress:** Ask, "What do you (or what does the team) want to get better at?"
- **Focus on student outcomes:** Encourage teachers to think about skills and standards—not about scores. The strongest teacher goals may require a change in classroom practice but must ultimately be connected to making improvements in student outcomes.
- **Ensure the goal is something that teachers can implement:** The goal should be within the teacher's sphere of influence and control. It should focus on actions or strategies that teachers can directly apply in their classrooms or professional practice, rather than on factors outside their control. This ensures that teachers feel empowered to make progress and can see a clear path to achieving their goals.

Researchers Amy Cassata and Elaine Allensworth (2021) note that skilled teachers working together in a building fosters a sense of collective efficacy. Cassata and Allensworth (2021) indicate, "it was not one person trying to enact change, but a team moving forward on a goal together" (p. 16).

Since performance goals (for example, SMART goals—strategic and specific, measurable, attainable, results oriented, and time bound [Conzemius & O'Neill, 2014]) have traditionally been the types of goals schools encourage, we are often asked (and sometimes challenged) about how to measure a mastery goal. We argue that they are measurable. For example, if the team's goal is to improve students' ability to develop, select, and apply better problem-solving strategies, the team might keep tallies of the different problem-solving strategies students use over time while monitoring for an increase in the variety and appropriateness of the strategies used. When the mastery goal involves a student learning need, teachers are already using measurement as part of their daily routines. In our experience, teachers do not find performance goals motivating, and we question whether teachers will ever accomplish goals they don't find meaningful. The following hypothetical example highlights how a teacher used mastery goals to improve literacy outcomes.

According to Hattie's Visible Learning synthesis (2023), mastery learning has an effect size of 0.67.

Determined to boost literacy outcomes for fourth-grade students in his class and across the cohort, a team leader led a process to reach consensus on the cohort's literacy goals. While keeping in mind the school's performance goal (half of the students achieving an A or B grade on an English assessment), the team leader encouraged his team to use on a mastery-oriented approach. The team identified two specific language skills crucial for the summative task: incorporating descriptive language and expressing opinions with textual evidence. Then they formulated a mastery goal: "Students will demonstrate proficiency in using descriptive language and evidence-based opinion writing in their texts." To measure progress toward this goal, the team regularly assessed student writing samples, tracked individual student growth in these two areas using rubrics, and provided opportunities for students to self-assess their language skills and set personal improvement goals. The mastery goal in this instance was providing enhanced opportunities for all students to build their knowledge of language features.

Rather than focusing exclusively on the performance measure, the teaching team looked to maximize opportunities to teach language features that support cohesive writing. Setting up peer-tutoring stations, teachers paired less proficient students with more able students to jointly construct model sentences. Teachers also taught students how to develop an opinion and to back it up with evidence. Sharing these opinions in a small group setting helped build confidence and bring out the best in the students.

According to Hattie's (2023) Visible Learning synthesis, peer tutoring has an effect size of 0.66.

Tapping Into the Sources of Efficacy

By collaborating to set mastery goals and work toward them, teachers can experience success and see the direct impact of their efforts on student learning, which contributes to their collective efficacy.

Here's what the team leader said.

> "Our team collaborated well together. We leveraged off each other's talents and shared resources within the cohort. While we initially focused on hitting a performance target, the more rewarding work was seeing students' faces light up when they received feedback from us about their cohesive writing. Knowing [the students'] improvement was as a result of our planning was a rewarding feeling."

Through this process, the team leader and all team members demonstrated that specific mastery goals were a powerful way to motivate each other.

The types of goals educators set can have a significant effect on their efficacy, satisfaction, motivation, and achievement. As noted earlier, this chapter's three micro-moves work in tandem. After teachers set mastery goals, the next step is to identify success criteria.

According to Hattie's (2023) Visible Learning synthesis, using success criteria in the classroom has an effect size of 0.64.

Identifying Success Criteria

In the classroom, criterion-based success (commonly referred to as *success criteria*) is used to help students engage in peer and self-assessment. When the criteria for success on learning objectives is more explicit, students can use that information to determine where they are in relation to the target. And with the right kind of feedback, students can then determine what they need to do to close the gap between where they currently are and where they need to be.

Using success criteria can also be an impactful strategy with teachers and teams, leading to school improvement. Helping teams determine what success looks like, based on a predetermined criterion, provides educators with a means to gauge progress toward mastery goals. Next, goal-referenced feedback helps teachers determine whether they are achieving their goals; seeing that they are making progress strengthens efficacy.

Principals can help teachers and teams identify success criteria based on identified student learning needs, teacher learning needs, or team learning needs. For example, if the target is to improve students' problem-solving abilities, a principal might engage a team in identifying the following success criteria.

- Students can define and clarify the problem.
- Students can determine the cause of the problem.
- Students can generate possible solutions.
- Students can prioritize, select, and implement a solution.
- Students can analyze the results to determine whether the resolution is producing the desired outcomes.

If the teacher's target is to improve their classroom management, a principal might engage the teacher in identifying the following success criteria.

- Students walk quietly into and out of the classroom.
- Students pay attention to signals for starting and stopping activities.
- Students place materials and supplies where they belong.
- Students pay attention to teachers' proximity and behave accordingly.

If a team has a target to increase students' desire to read in school, a principal might engage teacher teams in identifying the following success criteria.

- Students select the right reading material and carry books with them where they go.
- Students keep reading lists and track authors, series, and genres they enjoy.
- Students articulate connections between what they are reading and other interests.
- Students socialize around reading.
- Students are permitted and encouraged to abandon books they don't like.

These lists are not exhaustive but provide you with an idea of what success criteria for teachers' professional learning could sound like. Notice that each example is based on a learning need (learning to improve students' ability to problem solve, learning to improve classroom management techniques, and learning to increase the desire to read). Whatever the target, it's critical that the individual or the team considers the target important. Also, success criteria do not tell educators how to get there—figuring that out is where the learning takes place. Without clearly defined success criteria that answer the question "Where am I going?" it's difficult to determine how a team is doing in relation to the target.

Tapping Into the Sources of Efficacy

By clearly defining what success looks like in relation to their goals, monitoring their progress, and adjusting as needed, teachers ultimately experience a sense of accomplishment and increased collective efficacy when they achieve their targets.

One strategy for helping teachers identify success criteria is to co-construct them. Ask, "If we were to be successful with [insert target], what would that look like?" Help teachers envision the goal. How will they know that they have achieved their goal? What will be different in the school or classroom? What will they see and hear? How will they feel? Imagining what success will look like not only serves as a blueprint for monitoring the goal, but it also provides extra motivation, especially if the goal were self or team selected.

Providing Goal-Referenced Feedback

As the name suggests, *goal-referenced feedback* requires teachers to establish a goal and take action toward achieving it. The feedback is goal referenced in that it indicates to teachers and teacher teams whether they are on course or off track in achieving their goal. The purpose of goal-referenced feedback is not only to provide information about progress toward goals but also to recognize the team's achievements and offer guidance for improvement.

Some key characteristics of goal-referenced feedback include the following.

- **Specific:** The feedback is specific to the goals the team or teacher is pursuing rather than being general or vague.
- **Relevant:** The feedback is directly related to the actions, behaviors, or outcomes necessary for achieving the goals.
- **Timely:** Teachers and teams receive feedback in a timely manner, allowing them to make adjustments and improvements as needed.
- **Evidence-based:** The feedback is based on objective data, observations, or other evidence directly related to the goals.
- **Actionable:** The feedback includes clear, concrete suggestions for improvement or next steps for teachers and teams to move closer to their goals.

Goal-referenced feedback can be a powerful tool for supporting teacher growth and development. By connecting feedback to specific goals, such as mastery goals focused on developing skills and expertise, principals can help teachers understand how their work contributes to larger objectives. Connecting feedback to specific goals also provides teachers with targeted support for continuous improvement.

Tapping Into the Sources of Efficacy

By receiving feedback that is directly connected to their goals, teachers can better understand their progress, celebrate successes, and identify areas for improvement, ultimately experiencing a sense of accomplishment and increased collective efficacy as they work toward achieving their objectives.

For example, if a teacher team has set a mastery goal of improving their ability to use formative assessment to inform instruction, a principal might provide goal-referenced feedback by doing the following.

- Observing lessons and noting specific examples of how teachers are using formative assessment strategies
- Sharing data on student learning outcomes and discussing how formative assessment may have contributed to those results
- Offering suggestions for additional formative assessment techniques the team might try, based on best practices or professional learning resources
- Celebrating the team's progress in incorporating formative assessment and highlighting the impact on student learning

By consistently providing goal-referenced feedback, principals can help teachers maintain focus on their professional growth objectives, celebrate successes, and identify areas for ongoing development and support.

Tapping Into the Sources of Efficacy

"Learning environments that construe ability as an acquirable skill, deemphasize competitive social comparison, and highlight self-comparison of progress and personal accomplishments are well suited for building a sense of efficacy that promotes academic achievement" (Bandura, 1993, p. 125).

Collective Impact

When school leaders successfully prioritize measuring progress against predetermined criteria and overcome the detrimental effects of comparison, they create an environment where collective efficacy can flourish. By setting mastery goals, identifying criterion-based success, and providing goal-referenced feedback, principals can foster a culture of continuous learning, growth, and collaboration. School leaders have the power to shift the focus away from social comparison and toward individual and collective progress. By consistently emphasizing the importance of self-improvement and celebrating achievements based on agreed-on criteria, effective efficacy builders cultivate a sense of shared purpose and collective agency among teacher teams. Collective impact is realized when there is a commitment to personal and professional growth. By focusing on criteria-based success, principals create places where comparison is replaced by a shared sense of pride in individual and collective accomplishments, driving transformative change for all learners.

Comparison can be detrimental to efficacy, as it can interfere with the realization of mastery experiences. To overcome this, effective efficacy builders can help teachers measure progress against predetermined criteria rather than comparing themselves to others. The three micro-moves for doing so include setting mastery goals focused on learning and improvement, identifying criterion-based success criteria to gauge progress, and providing goal-referenced feedback that is specific, relevant, timely, evidence-based, and actionable. By emphasizing criteria over comparison, principals can foster a culture of continuous growth and collaboration, ultimately enhancing both individual and collective efficacy. Use the exercises and prompts in the reproducible "Planning for Action to Overcome Comparison" (page 132) to encourage teachers to focus on progress.

Planning for Action to Overcome Comparison

Use the following exercises to engage with the micro-moves discussed in chapter 8.

Setting Mastery Goals

Using the following guidelines, practice setting a mastery goal.

- **Focus on progress:** Ask, "What do you (or what does the team) want to get better at?"
- **Focus on student outcomes:** Encourage teachers to think about skills and standards—not about scores. The strongest teacher goals may require a change in classroom practice but must ultimately be connected to making improvements in student outcomes.
- **Ensure the goal is something that teachers can implement:** Encourage teachers to focus on actions or strategies that they can directly apply in their classrooms, rather than on factors outside their control.

Identifying Success Criteria

With colleagues, use the following questions to prompt discussion when identifying success criteria.

- If we were to be successful with [insert target], what would that look like?
- How will teachers know that they have achieved their goal?
- What will be different in the school or classroom?
- What will teachers see and hear if the goal is successful?
- How will teachers feel if they achieve their goal?

Providing Goal-Referenced Feedback

Use the following scenarios to practice providing goal-referenced feedback.

1. A teacher on your staff has the following mastery goal: "I want to improve my ability to facilitate student-led discussions to promote deeper understanding and critical thinking."

   Draft a piece of goal-referenced feedback based on the following scenario.

   During a classroom observation, you noticed that the teacher posed thought-provoking questions and allowed ample wait time for students to respond. However, only a few students participated in the discussion.

   Goal-referenced feedback:

2. A teacher on your staff has the following mastery goal: "I want to develop my skills in creating differentiated learning activities to meet the diverse needs of my students."

   Draft a piece of goal-referenced feedback based on the following scenario.

   In a lesson plan review, you found that the teacher included a variety of learning activities, but they did not seem to be tailored to students' specific readiness levels or learning preferences.

   Goal-referenced feedback:

3. A teacher on your staff has the following mastery goal: "I want to strengthen my ability to use formative assessment data to inform my instructional decisions."

   Draft a piece of goal-referenced feedback based on the following scenario.

   During a data team meeting, the teacher shared examples of formative assessments they had used, but struggled to articulate how they adjusted their instruction based on the results

   Goal-referenced feedback:

Chapter 9

Empowerment Over Hierarchy

By *developing teacher leaders,* school leaders can overcome *hierarchy* as an enemy of efficacy.

In this chapter, we examine how hierarchy becomes an enemy of efficacy. School leaders can overcome hierarchy by developing teacher leaders. Three key micro-moves leaders can turn to include validating informal leadership, expanding opportunities for formal teacher leadership, and increasing teacher autonomy and decision-making power. School leaders achieve collective impact as they empower teachers to lead and overcome the limitations of hierarchical structures.

Hierarchy as an Enemy of Efficacy

A *hierarchy* is a ranking of importance and power based on status or authority where each level is subordinate to the one above it. Hierarchy often creates a power imbalance because those at the top have more influence in making decisions that affect everyone in the building. In schools with very intense hierarchical structures, the experience for teachers can be quite challenging and potentially stressful. Leaders who use power and position to push an agenda or enforce compliance reduce teacher autonomy and motivation. Where a top-down culture exists, educators may grow concerned about the negative consequences if they speak up, question a proposal, or suggest alternative approaches. This fear can stifle creativity, innovation, and teachers' willingness to take risks. The intense power dynamics can lead to a culture of fear, conformity, and limited growth opportunities for teachers.

Hierarchies can also impede open lines of communication when multiple layers of red tape separate different levels within the school. In hierarchical structures, individuals often focus on their own goals rather than a collective agenda. This siloed mentality weakens collective efficacy because individual educators do not genuinely

> "Too much organizational control may deny teachers the very power and flexibility they need to do the job effectively, undermine their motivation, and squander a valuable human resource—the high degree of commitment of those who enter the teaching occupation" (Ingersoll, 2007, p. 24).

feel part of the collective. In hierarchical structures, teachers may feel undervalued, micromanaged, and unable to fully utilize their skills and expertise. For these reasons, hierarchy is an enemy of efficacy.

Since the early 2000s, many schools have moved toward more shared or distributed leadership approaches that emphasize collaboration, empowerment, and flexibility. However, hierarchical structures and command-and-control leadership are still found in some settings. And even though leadership styles have become more contemporary over time, the structure of schools has remained remarkably consistent. A typical medium-sized school will have one principal, a small number of assistant principals, heads of faculty, teaching staff, and often teaching assistants. This staffing mix is typically represented in a hierarchical format reflective of positions of authority and decision-making power. The principal sits at the top as the ultimate accountable officer within the school.

> "Command-and-control management is a hierarchical, top-down approach to management where decisions are made by those at the top of the organizational hierarchy and passed down to subordinates for implementation" (Jackson, 2023).

While this chain of command is helpful in outlining the structure of school leadership, achieving the power of collective impact requires that we challenge hierarchy by reframing teacher leadership. When school leaders leverage the skills, talents, and commitment of the collective rather than a select few, it goes a long way in fostering a sense of collective efficacy. Early efficacy research finds that reducing principals' hierarchy and control while empowering teachers through leadership, collaboration, and decision making increases teachers' sense of collective responsibility and efficacy beliefs (Lee, Dedrick, & Smith, 1991). Later research demonstrates similar findings. Researchers Mowafaq Qadach, Chen Schechter, and Rima Da'as (2019) conclude that by reducing hierarchical control and instead focusing on collaborative leadership approaches, principals can significantly impact teachers' collective beliefs about their ability to positively influence student outcomes. Teachers need to be able to see leadership shared and distributed among everyone within the school building—not just the principal or the leadership team.

To realize systemic and sustainable improvement in schools, principals can flatten hierarchy by empowering teachers within the building. Developing teachers as leaders empowers them to increase ownership and encourages the kind of innovation and creativity that results in mastery experiences. Environments where school leaders empower teachers lead to learning and growth. System and school leaders can take intentional steps to overcome hierarchy as an enemy of efficacy.

Overcoming Hierarchy by Developing Teacher Leaders

School principals can empower teachers and reduce the negative effects of hierarchy, thus realizing greater leadership from all educators, not just those with formal titles and responsibilities. By developing teachers as leaders, principals aim to flatten the hierarchy and strategically look for opportunities to empower the group. This is a critical component of the notion of collective impact. School leaders can overcome hierarchy by building capacity for teacher leadership and helping them to realize mastery experiences.

"The term school leader often brings to mind the school principal who works as a lone ranger. But no one leader has the resources of time, energy, and expertise to lead alone" (Spillane & Diamond, 2007, p. 8).

Teacher leadership is crucial for creating a collaborative and innovative learning environment that fosters collective efficacy and increases student success. Through an instructional leadership lens, teachers are in a unique position to assume responsibility for leading instructional improvement. When teachers see themselves as leaders of instructional improvement within their own classroom, among members of their grade or departments, and throughout the school, they become empowered. By influencing teachers to understand they have leadership potential that extends beyond their own classroom walls, principals capitalize on collective efforts.

Developing teachers as leaders can provide them with mastery experiences. When teachers successfully lead initiatives, facilitate professional learning, or mentor colleagues, they gain confidence in their abilities and are more likely to take on future leadership challenges. Efficacy increases as educators see the positive consequences of their own context-generated solutions.

For decades, educational thought leaders have promoted the benefits of teacher leadership. Ann Lieberman and Lynne Miller (2004) note that "teacher leaders are in a unique position to make change happen" (p. 12) and that teachers are "important change agents in meeting the new demands that schools face" (p. 12). Author, educator, and leadership consultant Douglas Reeves (2008) finds that "teachers not only exert significant influence on the performance of their students, but they also influence the performance of other teachers and school leaders" (p. 2). Education leaders Andrew Hargreaves and Michael Fullan (2012) assert that "teachers will always be more powerful than the principal" and that "successful and sustainable improvement can, therefore, never be done *to or even for* teachers. It can only ever be achieved *by and with them*" (p. 45). Finally, Derrington and Angelle (2013) state, "teacher leadership influences student achievement as well as school improvement efforts. The strong positive relationship between the constructs of teacher leadership and collective efficacy promotes success for students, teachers, and schools" (p. 6).

Leadership coach Jill Harrison Berg (2018) notes that "in schools, teacher leaders, including all teachers who share concern for students beyond their own classroom, are uniquely positioned to help their colleagues explore unconscious biases, adopt new professional practices, and translate classroom wisdom into equitable student-centered policies" (p. 84).

School systems also acknowledge the importance of teacher leadership. The Australian Institute for Teaching and School Leadership (AITSL, 2012) writes:

> Leadership must come from all levels, from those with and without formal leadership positions. A truly effective approach is characterized by a shared commitment to improvement and an acceptance that teachers have a powerful role to play in each other's development, as well as their own. (p. 5)

Research by education scholars Mary Lynne Derrington and Pamela S. Angelle (2013) shows a "clear and strong relationship between collective efficacy and the extent of teacher leadership in a school" (p. 6).

For teachers, this is particularly important as they must see a sense of influence and contribution toward school-improvement efforts. For principals, the importance of enabling and empowering teachers must be a skill set in their leadership repertoire.

James P. Spillane and John B. Diamond's research (2007) explores the concept of teacher leadership through a distributive perspective, in which "leadership is stretched over the work of multiple leaders" (p. 8). They characterize three different types of co-leading.

1. **Collaborated distribution:** This is characterized by multiple leaders working together at one time and place; for example, leading a faculty meeting.
2. **Collective distribution:** This highlights how the work of leaders performing separately can nonetheless be interdependent. For example, two assistant principals may divide the routine of classroom observations into a pedagogy focus and a behavior focus. In doing so, they work on the same leadership task at different times, but their work is interdependent.
3. **Coordinated distribution:** These are leadership routines that are performed in a sequence; for example, synthesizing data from the whole-school level for faculty leaders who then share these data during faculty meetings.

The intent of a distributed leadership approach is to harness the knowledge and expertise of multiple leaders in a way that far exceeds what individual leaders possess.

As noted earlier, empowering teachers by developing their leadership abilities matters for school success, not just for the individual who is taking on the role. As teachers in leadership roles model positive and productive behaviors, they become vicarious sources of efficacy for their colleagues. When teacher leaders support experimentation and risk taking that result in mastery moments, they provide the pathway to collective efficacy. Three micro-moves for developing teacher leaders include (1) validating informal leadership, (2) expanding opportunities for formal leadership, and (3) increasing teacher autonomy and decision-making power.

Research by Jennifer York-Barr and Karen Duke (2004) shows that teacher leadership is positively associated with student achievement, teacher retention, and overall school effectiveness.

Adams and Forsyth (2006) demonstrate that when the conditions are set for teachers to come together to determine solutions to challenges of practices and hierarchy is flattened, it fosters a sense of collective efficacy.

Validating Informal Leadership

Teacher leadership can manifest in many different forms. Some leadership positions are officially designated with specific duties and titles (for example, mentor-teacher, instructional coach, or curriculum specialist). Others arise naturally and informally through teachers' daily interactions with their colleagues (for example, teachers sharing instructional strategies, modeling professional curiosity and growth, or advocating for under-served students). Lieberman and Miller (2005) spent decades studying teachers as leaders and find that among the many roles and responsibilities teachers can assume, three appeared to be critical: (1) advocating for a profession that perceives itself as a collaborative intellectual endeavor, (2) upholding high standards, and (3) advocating for new forms of accountability. These three critical roles underscore the importance of validating informal leadership since they can be carried out by *anyone* in the profession and are not reserved for only those who hold official titles.

"There is no loss of power and influence on the part of headteachers when . . . the power and influence of many others in the school increase" (Leithwood, Harris, & Hopkins, 2008, p. 39).

Teachers often do not recognize, however, that they are assuming leadership when it's informal in nature. By validating leadership that has emerged organically, principals honor the valuable contributions teachers make every day. By acknowledging, appreciating, and making explicit what informal leadership looks like, principals can help teachers see their leadership potential and encourage more teachers to step up. When principals recognize and encourage informal leadership efforts, they create an environment where all educators feel equipped to make a meaningful impact on student learning and school success.

"If we continue to accept that leaders are only those with formal titles and responsibilities who manage or control others, then we continue to exclude, rather than include, most people who are leading in their lives and workplaces" (Ferguson, 2023, p. 51).

Tapping Into the Sources of Efficacy

Validating informal leadership in a school can lead to mastery experiences by acknowledging and celebrating the everyday efforts and successes of teachers who take initiative and positively influence their colleagues. By publicly recognizing these informal leadership actions, principals help teachers become aware of their own leadership potential, boosting their confidence and sense of collective efficacy in driving school improvement.

Some strategies for validating informal leadership include the following.

- Leaders can expand teachers' understanding and recognition of the various ways in which they can demonstrate leadership outside formally designated roles.
- Leaders can make teachers aware of how they lead by example every day through their words, actions, and behaviors.
- Leaders can look for instances where teachers are taking initiative and publicly acknowledge and appreciate these efforts.
- Leaders can regularly showcase examples of informal teacher leadership during staff meetings, acknowledging specific individuals and their contributions.
- Leaders can work with informal teacher leaders to define their roles, responsibilities, and goals.
- Leaders can send personalized notes of appreciation to informal teacher leaders, recognizing their efforts and impact on the school community.
- Leaders can ensure that informal teacher leaders have access to the resources and support they need to be effective.
- Leaders can provide informal teacher leaders with access to leadership-focused professional development opportunities.
- Leaders can extend leadership opportunities by inviting informal teacher leaders to participate in schoolwide committees, lead professional development sessions, or represent the school at district-level events. We expand on this in the following section.

When principals use the micro-move of validating informal leadership, they help create a culture of shared leadership and collaboration.

Expanding Opportunities for Formal Teacher Leadership

Another micro-move for developing teacher leaders is to expand opportunities for teachers to take on formal leadership roles. When system and school leaders do so, they create a more structured and intentional approach to teacher leadership within districts and schools. This expansion may include creating new leadership positions or reviewing and revising existing ones, such as department chairs or grade-level team leaders. Cindy Harrison and Joellen Killion (2007) of Learning Forward outline different ways that teacher leaders can contribute to their school's success. These include acting as a data coach, facilitating professional learning, mentoring, demonstrating lessons, observing peers and providing feedback, and serving on committees.

Based on the context and needs within their buildings, principals could identify opportunities for leadership. Is there a need for a community liaison or equity champion? Are teachers being asked to implement a new program or curriculum? If so, perhaps there is a need for an implementation supporter. Is there a need for a well-being advocate or social-emotional lead? How are teachers currently integrating technology? Perhaps a teacher could fill the role as a technology specialist. Is there a need to increase student involvement in the school? If so, could a teacher take on the role of student voice amplifier? By creating a variety of roles, principals allow teachers to discover leadership opportunities that align with their strengths and passions.

Tapping Into the Sources of Efficacy

Expanding opportunities for formal teacher leadership can contribute to mastery experiences and collective efficacy by providing structured pathways for teachers to take on defined leadership roles that align with their strengths and the school's needs.

Principals can also establish a leadership pipeline that demonstrates a clear pathway for teachers to move from informal to formal leadership roles. This entails identifying teachers who demonstrate strong leadership potential, clearly communicating the various formal leadership roles available within the school, and establishing a clear and transparent application and selection process. Also, it's important to recognize that teacher leaders need ongoing support and mentoring to move into formal leadership roles as they navigate challenges, build relationships, and continue to grow and develop as leaders. Finally, principals can work with teacher leaders to develop long-term succession plans, identifying potential future leaders and providing them with the necessary support and preparation to eventually step into teacher leadership roles. Ultimately, by establishing a leadership pipeline, principals demonstrate a commitment to investing in the long-term success and sustainability of school improvement. By empowering teacher leaders, principals create the conditions for collective teacher efficacy and ultimately realize better outcomes for all students.

Increasing Teacher Autonomy and Decision-Making Power

In *Outliers: The Story of Success*, author Malcolm Gladwell (2008) offers three qualities that work must have to be satisfying: (1) autonomy, (2) complexity, and (3) a connection between reward and effort. Gladwell (2008) suggests that meaningful work (such as teaching) fulfills all three criteria. Author Daniel H. Pink (2009) also shares research on the motivating factors employees look for to drive their performance and notes that autonomy is one of the key factors that drives intrinsic motivation. According to Pink's (2009) synthesis of the research on motivation, providing individuals with autonomy in their work can lead to increased engagement, creativity, and performance.

When teachers have greater autonomy, they are more likely to take ownership of their practice and make positive changes in their classrooms, schools, and communities. When teachers have autonomy over decisions related to instructional methods, they are more likely to experiment with new strategies, technologies, and approaches to teaching and learning. Autonomy also allows teachers to identify their own professional learning needs and pursue opportunities for growth and development. Teachers with autonomy are more likely to step into leadership roles and collaborate with their colleagues to improve schoolwide practices and policies. When teachers have the autonomy to make decisions in the best interests of their students, they are more likely to advocate for resources, support, and opportunities that promote student success (Qianggiang, 2021).

Roger Goddard (2002) finds that when teachers have the opportunity to influence important, instructionally relevant school decisions, they also tend to have stronger beliefs in the combined ability of the faculty to positively impact student achievement.

We're not suggesting that teachers become completely independent contractors. Pink (2009) makes a clear distinction between autonomy and independence. He asserts that autonomy means "acting with choice—which means we can be both autonomous and happily interdependent with others" (p. 90). Fullan and Hargreaves (2016) use the term *collective autonomy*, which they describe as teachers having "more independence from unnecessary and excessive bureaucratic interference but also less independence from one another as colleagues in planning curriculum, improving teaching and learning, and giving as well as receiving feedback" (p. 19).

Tapping Into the Sources of Efficacy

Increasing teacher autonomy and decision-making power can lead to mastery experiences by empowering teachers to take ownership of their practice, experiment with new strategies, and make decisions that best support their students' needs.

Autonomy also does not mean lack of accountability. The principal can still set clear expectations and provide feedback, but they do so in a way that encourages dialogue and collaboration rather than top-down directives. By structuring the conditions for greater collective autonomy, school leaders provide teachers with decision-making power on how, when, and with whom teachers conduct their work, as long as they meet certain standards and goals. When school leaders ensure that teachers make the decisions about how they design and deliver instruction, assess student learning, and manage their classrooms, all within the framework of school and district guidelines and expectations, teachers will feel empowered. With permission to make instructional decisions, teachers use this power to positively enhance outcomes. Rather than waiting for a directive from above, teachers can generate solutions they can trial and test directly in their classrooms.

Educational management scholar Philip Hallinger (2003) advises, "leadership must be conceptualized as a mutual influence process rather than as a one-way process in which leaders influence others" (p. 346).

Principals can increase teacher autonomy and decision-making power in the following ways.

- Offer teachers leadership roles that extend beyond their classrooms.
- Provide teachers freedom to select and implement evidence-based strategies that best suit their students' learning needs.
- Establish teacher-led professional learning where teachers can share best practices and make collective decisions about strategies and school policies.
- Provide teachers with discretionary funds or more say in budget allocation.

In summary, teacher autonomy and decision-making power are mutually reinforcing aspects of teacher professionalism and empowerment. The degree of autonomy shapes the decisions teachers can make, while the scope of decision-making power determines the bounds of autonomy. Striking the right balance and providing support are key to realizing the benefits of teacher autonomy for educators and students.

Collective Impact

When school leaders successfully empower teachers and overcome the limitations of hierarchical structures, they create an environment where collective efficacy can flourish. By validating informal leadership, expanding opportunities for formal leadership roles, and increasing teacher autonomy and decision-making power, principals foster a culture of shared ownership, collaboration, and continuous improvement. School leaders can tap into the collective wisdom and expertise of their teams, recognizing that leadership is not confined to those with formal titles but is distributed throughout the school community. By consistently communicating the value of teacher leadership and providing opportunities for teachers to take on meaningful roles, effective efficacy builders will cultivate a sense of collective responsibility and agency among their staff. Collective impact can only be realized when teachers feel a sense of empowerment. In facilitating teacher leadership, principals create places where hierarchy is replaced by a shared sense of purpose, a willingness to collaborate, and a deep belief in the power of collective efficacy to transform student outcomes.

In exploring the research on achieving collective impact, we found some dominant and consistent themes. In schools with high levels of collective efficacy, the principal and other school leaders fostered a culture that empowered teachers while developing teacher leadership. We began this chapter highlighting how the hierarchy within a school can be an enemy of collective efficacy. With teachers leading the way, both individual and collective efficacy can increase. School leadership then broadens from a linear hierarchical model to a model dense with leadership throughout every layer. The concept of shared ownership becomes the norm and high levels of collaboration foster improved student learning and well-being outcomes. Irrespective of the specific roles they undertake, teacher leaders make a significant impact by helping to shape mastery environments where everyone in an educational setting believes they have the individual and collective capability to impact positive outcomes.

Hierarchy is an enemy of efficacy because of the way it can impede progress, limit creativity, and slow momentum. Collective efficacy is more challenging to cultivate when teachers don't have authentic opportunities to lead the work of school improvement. Effective efficacy builders can overcome hierarchy by using their repertoire of instructional leadership skills to full effect. Techniques to overcome hierarchy and promote agency provided in this chapter include validating informal leaders, expanding opportunities for formal leadership, and increasing teacher autonomy and decision-making power. Use the exercises and prompts in the reproducible "Planning for Action to Overcome Hierarchy" (page 146) to develop teacher leaders.

Planning for Action to Overcome Hierarchy

Use the following exercises to engage with the micro-moves discussed in chapter 9.

Validating Informal Leadership

List five to ten examples of informal teacher leadership you've observed in your school. These could include teachers sharing instructional strategies, advocating for students, or demonstrating professional growth.

Group the examples into categories based on the type of leadership demonstrated (for example, instructional leadership, student advocacy, or professional growth).

For each category, brainstorm two to three specific ways you can acknowledge and appreciate these informal leadership efforts. Consider strategies like public acknowledgment, personalized notes, or showcasing examples during staff meetings.

Expanding Opportunities for Formal Leadership

Follow these steps to expand opportunities for formal leadership.

1. Review current leadership roles.
   a. In the space provided, list all existing formal teacher leadership roles within the school, such as department chairs, grade-level team leaders, or instructional coaches. For each role, briefly describe the key responsibilities and impact on school improvement efforts.

Formal Leadership Roles	Key Responsibilities	Impact on School Improvement Efforts

2. Identify areas for expansion.
   a. Brainstorm areas where additional teacher leadership could support school goals and student success. Consider areas such as data analysis, technology integration, equity and inclusion, or family engagement.
   b. For each area, list potential leadership roles or responsibilities that could be assigned to teachers.
3. Develop role descriptions.
   a. For each prioritized leadership role, create a detailed description that outlines the key responsibilities, qualifications, and expectations.

4. Create a selection process.
    a. Determine the criteria and process for selecting teachers for each leadership role.
    b. Communicate the opportunities and selection process to all teachers and invite applications or nominations.
    c. Convene a committee of administrators and teacher leaders to review applications and make selections.
5. Provide support and resources.
    a. Identify the professional learning, mentoring, and resources needed to support teachers in their new leadership roles.
    b. Develop a plan for providing ongoing professional development and support to teacher leaders.
    c. Allocate time, budget, and other resources to ensure that teacher leaders have the capacity to fulfill their responsibilities.

Increasing Teacher Autonomy and Decision-Making Power

Follow these steps to increase teacher autonomy and decision-making power.

1. Assess current levels of autonomy.
    a. List the key areas of teacher practice, such as curriculum, instruction, assessment, and professional learning.
    b. For each area, rate the current level of teacher autonomy and decision-making power on a scale of 1 through 5, with 1 representing low levels of autonomy and decision-making power and 5 indicating high levels.
    c. Identify areas where teacher autonomy is currently low and could be increased.
2. Brainstorm opportunities for increased autonomy.
    a. For each area identified in step 1, brainstorm specific ways to increase teacher autonomy and decision-making power.
    b. Consider strategies such as teacher-led collaborative teams, choice in professional learning, flexibility in curriculum and assessment, and input on school policies and procedures.
    c. Be sure to consider the potential benefits and challenges of each idea.
3. Develop an implementation plan.
    a. For each high-priority idea, identify the specific actions needed to put the idea into practice, along with timelines, resources, and responsibilities.
    b. Consider how to communicate the changes to teachers and other stakeholders, and how to support teachers in their new roles and responsibilities.

Part 4

Vicarious Experiences

Vicarious experiences are a powerful source of collective efficacy. In addition to the three other sources, teachers also rely on vicarious experiences to provide vital information to shape their collective efficacy beliefs. These experiences happen when educators see others who are faced with similar challenges and opportunities perform well. When educators visualize themselves in the shoes of others who have had success, they become convinced that they too have what it takes. Principals play a pivotal role in encouraging vicarious experiences. Leaders are key figures in mobilizing resources and creating the conditions to put teachers together to learn vicariously, develop, and grow.

Vicarious experiences move beyond social interactions or simply connecting teachers in collaborative teams. Vicarious experiences are more than just observations; they're observations with intention. They have a clear purpose and have a close connection to the important work of improving student learning outcomes. For educators plagued by self-doubt, connecting vicariously can provide the necessary boost to efficacy levels. One of the most effective ways of generating vicarious experiences is through modeling and discussion.

Modeling is a powerful tool that goes beyond simply demonstrating skills. Teachers actively seek out and learn from colleagues who excel in areas where they want to improve. For instance, a new teacher might observe a veteran educator's classroom management techniques to enhance their own practice. Principals who want to build collective efficacy in their schools should use modeling strategically to promote learning among their staff.

Effective modeling isn't limited to visual demonstrations; it also includes verbal communication and actions. For example, when an experienced teacher shares a story during a staff meeting about overcoming a challenging student behavior issue with determination and hope, they're not just telling an anecdote: They're modeling resilience and problem solving for their colleagues. Similarly, when a team of teachers presents how they persevered through initial setbacks to successfully implement a new reading program, they're providing a vicarious experience of confidence and persistence for the entire staff. These examples of overcoming obstacles can inspire and motivate other educators, reinforcing the belief that they too can surmount difficulties in their own classrooms.

In the three chapters in part 4, we identify three enemies of efficacy: isolation, ambiguity, and fragmentation. We then offer a range of micro-moves promoting vicarious experiences to overcome them. By strategically integrating vicarious experiences, principals create prime opportunities to deepen collaborative connections and create meaningful impact. A principal can effectively orchestrate vicarious experience by increasing interdependencies, fostering consensus building, and focusing on implementation.

In part 4, we discuss the following micro-moves.

- By *extending invitations to say more*, school leaders can realize a deeper level of understanding when exploring a problem. Using this micro-move, educators create the space for joint problem solving and increase collective responsibility for the outcome.
- By *helping teams to set interdependent goals*, principals can help educators understand that everyone plays a part in achieving collective impact.
- By *engaging teams in interdependent tasks*, educators develop stronger connections as they deepen levels of trust between team members.
- By *guiding an affinity-mapping process*, principals garner support for policy as they determine whether teachers are in favor of the new policy and what burning questions they may have.
- By *using the realm of concern versus the realm of influence protocol*, principals can guide teachers to create an action plan focused on the things they're able to influence.
- By *analyzing student work samples*, principals and teachers can form a shared understanding of their students' learning needs and reach consensus on the next steps.
- By *gatekeeping*, the principal keeps the main focus as the main focus. This avoids distractions and focuses on what's important.
- By *applying the 80–20 principle,* educators come to identify and focus only on the things that will deeply enhance student outcomes.
- Finally, by *prioritizing evidence-based practices*, principals and teachers boost efficacy levels by realizing positive progress in student learning outcomes.

Chapter 10

Interdependence Over Isolation

By *increasing interdependencies*, school leaders can overcome *isolation* as an enemy of efficacy.

In this chapter, we look at how isolation becomes an enemy of efficacy. School leaders can overcome isolation by increasing interdependencies. Three key micro-moves leaders can turn to include extending invitations to say more, helping teams set interdependent goals, and engaging teams in interdependent tasks. School leaders achieve collective impact as they overcome isolation by fostering interdependence.

Isolation as an Enemy of Efficacy

Isolation describes the experience of being separated from others, often with limited social contact or support. For example, teachers can choose to be isolated within their school by simply closing their classroom doors. They may do this to retain a sense of privacy or freedom from scrutiny. Faculties within a high school can isolate themselves from other departments by not sharing new strategies they have tried with their students. School leaders can also choose to isolate themselves by not connecting with neighboring schools or participating in district-led initiatives designed to improve the system. There may be a variety of reasons educators and leaders choose to do this. The point is that isolation will likely affect levels of collective efficacy.

Isolation can also be by circumstance when it is created by distance. In the United States, scores of smaller schools in rural and remote areas can experience a sense of geographic isolation. The same is true in remote locations in Australia and Canada, where schools may be isolated by extreme weather conditions and vast distances. In these situations, school teams need to be wary of the risk of isolation and pay attention to strategies to ensure educators retain a sense of connection to internal and external school teams.

Teacher isolation has been an ongoing issue since it was first researched in the 1970s. In 1975, education professor Dan Lortie wrote an influential book called *Schoolteacher: A Sociological Study*. In this study, he identifies teacher isolation as a major structural barrier to improving student learning in schools. He notes that for nearly two centuries, the dominant model of teaching involved teachers working independently in their own classrooms, rarely collaborating or sharing practices with colleagues. This isolation, Lortie (1975) argues, was deeply entrenched in organizational structures, which included the way schools are laid out physically, and in the culture of schools, due to limited opportunities for teachers to observe each other's practice or engage in professional dialogue.

"Enhancing collective efficacy through professional learning remains a challenge as teachers commonly express feelings of isolation, despite working within rich and interactive social contexts" (Beauchamp, Klassen, Parsons, Durksen, & Taylor, 2014, p. 48).

According to Lortie (1975), this isolation has several negative consequences. It impedes the spread of effective teaching practices, as successful strategies often remained confined to individual classrooms. It also makes it difficult for novice teachers to learn from experienced colleagues. Without collaboration, teachers must rely on trial and error to improve their teaching practice.

Fifteen years after Lortie's study, researcher Judith Warren Little (1990) published a seminal article for the teaching profession titled "The Persistence of Privacy." Little (1990) notes that despite various efforts to foster teacher collaboration, the norms of privacy and noninterference among teachers remained strong in schools. Like Lortie, Little finds that the culture of isolation was sustained by both organizational factors (for example, school architecture and scheduling) and teachers' own preferences for autonomy and privacy. Little (1990) indicates that teachers tend to work independently in their classrooms and are hesitant to share practices, observe each other, or engage in substantive professional dialogue.

In the decades since these publications, many districts and schools have made efforts to break down teacher isolation through professional learning communities, instructional coaching, team teaching, and other collaborative structures. However, findings from studies in the 2010s reveal that teacher isolation remains a significant problem in many schools, negatively impacting job satisfaction, professional growth, and student learning (Ostovar-Namaghi & Sheikhahmadi, 2016). In a study published in 2014, researchers Ana Maria Forte and Maria Assunção Flores report that teacher collaboration is often limited to superficial exchanges of materials or ideas rather than deeper forms of collaborative inquiry and joint problem solving. They also find that barriers to collaboration include lack of time, scheduling constraints, and a persistent culture of individualism among teachers. Education scholar David J. Flinders (2019) provides an updated review of the state of teacher isolation, confirming that it remains a significant challenge, particularly at the secondary level, despite decades of reform efforts.

Flinders (2019) reports that one factor contributing to teacher isolation is a lack of leadership support for collaboration. He emphasizes the importance of school-level factors and leadership in creating the conditions for teachers to work together effectively.

The very nature of collective efficacy implies that there's a *collective*. Therefore, isolation, whether through circumstance or deliberate choice, is an enemy of efficacy. When educators attempt to tackle a challenge on their own or work in individualistic ways, they miss the opportunity to learn and grow vicariously. Educational leadership scholar Richard F. Elmore (2000) states, "privacy of practice produces isolation; isolation is the enemy of improvement" (p. 20). A culture of privacy does not produce the desired conditions whereby educators can learn, reflect, and grow from one other. The power of collective efficacy is lost if opportunities to break the impact of isolation are not realized. We learned earlier that vicarious experiences are a key source of collective efficacy. For this reason, isolation is an enemy of efficacy.

Researchers Jacqueline Schlichte, Nina Ysseel, and John Merbler (2005) conducted a qualitative study examining teacher isolation through case studies. They find that factors contributing to teacher isolation include lack of collaboration time, becoming detached from colleagues, and feeling overwhelmed with responsibilities.

The intent of this chapter is not to say that teachers must complete everything as a team. We recognize that for some tasks, it is far more efficient to complete them individually. However, if the goal is leveraging the power of collective efficacy to lift student learning, an increase in interdependence is a must.

We also want to acknowledge that there are many promising examples of districts and schools that have successfully fostered teacher collaboration and increased interdependencies among teachers. These schools are often characterized by strong professional learning communities, supportive leadership, and a culture of collective responsibility.

Collaboration is most effective when the task or problem is so complex, it would be too difficult to work on alone (Donohoo & Anderson, 2022).

To realize systemic and sustainable improvements in schools, principals can find ways to foster interdependence and efficacy. Fostering the belief that educators can and do make a difference in the learning lives of students is an important focus for school leaders. Isolation prevents leaders from capitalizing on the efficacy-enhancing nature of vicarious experiences; therefore, the need to reduce isolation is important. Environments where interdependence is privileged over isolation contribute to learning and growth. System and school leaders can take intentional steps to overcome isolation as an enemy of efficacy.

Overcoming Isolation With Interdependence

School principals can overcome isolation even though its legacy persists in many contexts and even when fully overcoming isolation remains an ongoing challenge for school leaders seeking to maximize student learning. Breaking down the barriers isolation creates and fostering a sense of collective efficacy happen when educators work in interdependent ways and reduce the negative impact that isolation can have. School leaders can overcome isolation by taking deliberate steps to increase interdependencies.

The collective working memory effect suggests that if the task complexity exceeds the limits of an individual's working memory, then working in a team is more effective (Kirschner, Sweller, Kirschner, & Zambrano, 2018).

Interdependence is a defining characteristic of effective teamwork. As noted earlier, even though Little's (1990) article was published decades ago, the concepts described are still very relevant in schools today. Little (1990) provides a continuum in which she describes the progressive shifts from conditions of complete independence to interdependence. At the independent end, "teacher autonomy rests on freedom from scrutiny and the largely unexamined right to exercise personal preference. . . . Independent trial and error serves as the principal route to competence" (Little, 1990, p. 513). She introduces the term *joint work* at the opposite end of the continuum. Joint work rests on the *shared* responsibility for the work of teaching. Little (1990) shares, "joint work anticipates truly collective action—teachers' decisions to pursue a single course of action in concert or, alternatively, to decide on a set of basic priorities that in turn guide the independent choices of individual teachers" (p. 519).

The relationship between collective efficacy and performance is maximized when team members are interdependent. In a meta-analysis that examines the relationship between efficacy and performance, researchers Stanley M. Gully, Kara A. Incalcaterra, Aparna Joshi, and J. Matthew Beauien (2002) conclude, "When the task and context encourage coordination, communication, and cooperation among members, team-efficacy is related more strongly to performance than when interdependence is low" (p. 827). To capitalize on the relationship between efficacy and performance, it is beneficial to increase interdependencies among teachers and teams. Three micromoves that principals can use to take intentional steps to overcome isolation as an enemy of efficacy include (1) extending invitations to say more, (2) helping teams set interdependent goals, and (3) engaging teams in interdependent tasks.

Extending Invitations to Say More

Little (as cited in Crow, 2008) is also well known for her work in studying professional learning communities and, in particular, teachers' conversations. With an interest in whether and how ordinary workplace interactions afford sustained attention to problems of practice and experiences in the classroom, Little (as cited in Crow, 2008) provides the following great insights.

- Three things often occur when a problem of practice is identified: it's ignored, joked about, or deflected.
- When a problem of practice is noticed, it gets normalized: "the issue is recognized as an ordinary, expected, and shared problem of the classroom" (Crow, 2008, p. 55). Teachers then provide reassurance and empathy or offer advice.

How can teachers shift these interactions? Little (as cited in Crow, 2008) identifies a simple strategy that results in conversations developing in rich ways—an invitation to *say more*. Little notes, "the invitation to say more is one of the things that marked a learning rich conversation" (Crow, 2008, p. 55). Rather than stopping at reassurance or moving quickly to a remedy, when teachers are invited to say more, it's more likely that the nature of the problem gets unpacked, and the conversation yields more than a quick fix. Consider the following benefits of the strategy.

- When teachers have more intimate knowledge about what goes on inside each other's classrooms, they are better positioned to engage in conversations that convey enough specificity to better understand problems of practice.
- When teachers share a curriculum and understandings about particular instructional approaches, it creates opportunities for greater interdependence.

Tapping Into the Sources of Efficacy

Inviting teachers to say more about their classroom experiences can lead to vicarious experiences as they share specific details about successes and challenges. As teachers gain more intimate knowledge of each other's classrooms through these conversations, they can better relate to and learn from one another's experiences, building a shared sense of collective efficacy.

Principals can use this simple micro-move of extending invitations to say more to increase collaboration and cooperation among teachers. As teachers share specifics about problems of practice, they create space for joint problem solving and increase collective responsibility for the outcome. By discussing successes and failures, while recognizing interdependence among team members, educators can collectively take credit or be held accountable. The micro-move of extending invitations to say more allows teachers more intimate knowledge of each other's classrooms and better positions team members to provide helpful insights while engaged in joint work.

Helping Teams Set Interdependent Goals

In schools, greater interdependence occurs when teachers work together toward a common goal. Rather than keeping to themselves, teachers collaborate and facilitate efforts to progress toward shared interests. Interdependent goals promote shared responsibility and imply collective action. Everyone's contributions and efforts are needed to achieve interdependent goals. In addition, when teams recognize that their current actions are not helping them progress toward their goals, they devise better strategies to get them there.

For example, a team of ninth-grade teachers shared a common concern. They noticed that many of their students were experiencing difficulties with proportional reasoning in mathematics and addressing the students' learning needs became the focus of the team's joint work. To help students build on their knowledge of quantities and how they relate to each other, the team set the following interdependent goal: All ninth graders will be able to accurately represent proportional relationships in tables, equations, graphs, and written and verbal descriptions.

By deconstructing the mathematics standards and co-creating lessons over time, the teachers were able to draw on each other's knowledge and expertise. By observing the delivery of the co-created lessons and resulting student outcomes, both misconceptions and eureka moments, the teachers were able to gain a greater understanding of what students were experiencing. By debriefing as a team, the teachers were able to refine their teaching strategies and make improvements to their individual practice. As a result, their students' understanding increased and the team realized measurable improvements in their students' achievement.

Teachers' efficacy beliefs and their expectations about what their students could accomplish increased as well. A teacher reported, "When I saw what the others had their students doing, I thought 'my kids can't do that.' Through our work, though, I've realized that's not true. I'm also more confident now contributing to joint lesson planning." This is the type of learning experience all teachers deserve and school leaders can help make it happen through interdependent goal setting.

Researchers Aitor Aritzeta and Nekane Balluerka (2006) find that over time, goal interdependence becomes a strong predictor for cooperation within teams.

Tapping Into the Sources of Efficacy

According to Bandura (1997), vicarious experiences are one of the main sources that influence teacher efficacy beliefs. Vicarious experiences like the one described here become important sources of efficacy for individuals and teams.

Aritzeta and Balluerka (2006) find that the fit between personal and team goals is a critical feature for team effectiveness. When individual and group goals appear together, they increase motivational outcomes.

Engaging Teams in Interdependent Tasks

The second type of interdependence, *task interdependence*, refers to how well connected teachers are based on the tasks they engage in while working collaboratively. Some tasks require very little interdependence. For example, when planning events, like a community mathematics night, teachers usually take on individual roles and assignments. One teacher might create a community invitation, another gathers manipulatives, and another takes on the task of ordering snacks and beverages. While coordinated efforts are important in this example and help to ensure greater efficiency, interdependence is reduced when teachers approach tasks with the intent to "divide and conquer."

In an experiment designed to test the relationship between performance and interdependence, researchers Tal Y. Katz-Navon and Miriam Erez (2005) find that when team tasks, goals, and outcomes require lower levels of interdependence, the relationship between collective efficacy and performance is minimized. Under conditions of low task interdependence, collective efficacy has no significance. Katz-Navon and Erez's (2005) research validates task interdependence as a necessary condition for the emergence of collective efficacy.

Tasks that require a high degree of interdependence, on the other hand, help to strengthen collective efficacy. Returning to the example from the ninth-grade team of teachers, they collaborated on designing, delivering, and debriefing lessons. In doing so, they drew on each other's experiences and expertise, pooling ideas, methods, and materials. They examined their practices publicly, gained new knowledge and skills through trial and error, feedback, and reflection based on evidence. They engaged in joint decision making on matters of teaching, learning, and assessing.

Tapping Into the Sources of Efficacy

As teachers work closely together, pooling their knowledge, skills, and resources to jointly make decisions and solve problems, they gain valuable insights from observing and learning from each other's successes and challenges.

Leaders can structure tasks that require greater interdependence by providing opportunities for teachers to plan, deliver, and debrief lessons based on identified student learning needs. They can do this in several ways. One idea is to implement a lesson study approach where a team of teachers collaboratively plans a lesson, one teaches it while others observe, and then the group debriefs and refines the lesson. Another way principals can increase interdependencies is by facilitating interdisciplinary projects that require teachers from different subject areas to work together, aligning their curricula and instruction. Principals can also task teams of teachers with creating common assessments, ensuring alignment across classrooms and promoting shared expectations. If distance is an issue, online platforms can connect teachers so that they can engage in joint work.

Collective Impact

When school leaders successfully foster interdependence and overcome the detrimental effects of isolation, they create an environment where collective efficacy can thrive. By extending invitations to say more, helping teams set interdependent goals, and engaging teams in interdependent tasks, principals can cultivate a culture of collaboration, shared responsibility, and continuous improvement. School leaders can break down the barriers that keep teachers isolated in their classrooms and create opportunities for meaningful, purposeful collaboration. By consistently modeling and facilitating joint work, effective efficacy builders will foster a sense of collective ownership and agency among their staff, as they recognize that their individual success is contingent on the efforts of the entire team. Collective impact is dependent on teachers' interdependence. When principals create the conditions for collaboration and joint work, schools become places where isolation is replaced by a shared sense of purpose, a willingness to learn from and with one another, and a deep belief in the power of collective efficacy to transform student outcomes.

Isolation is an enemy of efficacy because it prevents leaders from making the most of the efficacy-enhancing nature of vicarious experiences. People working in isolation—within schools, across school districts, or among school community groups—it prevents having a shared language and taking action that might otherwise facilitate productive collaboration. Realizing the impact of collective efficacy means harnessing the power of the collective. Effective efficacy builders can overcome isolation by creating the conditions for joint work. Joint work, according to Little (1990), moves beyond storytelling to aiding, assisting, and sharing ideas, methods, and opinions. Joint work is characterized by teachers' collective action and a level of interdependence where individual success is contingent on the efforts of the entire team. The relationship between collective efficacy and performance is maximized when there is positive interdependence among team members (Gully et al., 2002). Micro-moves to increase interdependencies in this chapter include extending invitations to say more, helping teams set interdependent goals, and engaging teams in interdependent tasks. Use the exercises and prompts in the reproducible "Planning for Action to Overcome Isolation" (page 160) to practice increasing interdependence among teachers.

Planning for Action to Overcome Isolation

Use the following exercises to engage with the micro-moves discussed in chapter 10.

Extending Invitations to Say More

Before the next team meeting, ask teachers to come prepared with a recent classroom challenge they've faced. Briefly explain the concept of *extending invitations to say more* and its benefits. Place teachers in triads and ask teachers to take turns sharing their classroom challenge. Those who are listening should ask open-ended questions and prompts to invite the teacher who is sharing to elaborate. For example, "Can you tell me more about that?" or "What do you think led to this situation?" After teachers have all had an opportunity to share, debrief with the larger group by posing the following questions.

- How did it feel to be invited to say more?
- What new insights did you gain while listening to other people's experiences?
- How did this experience differ from typical problem-solving conversations?
- How can we incorporate this practice into our regular team meetings?

Helping Teams Set Interdependent Goals

Use the following questions to collectively brainstorm ideas to strengthen the goal-setting process by creating interdependent goals (that is, goals that are connected and reliant on each team member playing their part).

- What is our shared (interdependent) goal?

- What are our shared responsibilities? (What are we all responsible for?)

- What are our collective actions? (What are the actions we are collectively committing to?)

- What are our vicarious experiences? (How are we going to connect vicariously?)

Engaging Teams in Interdependent Tasks

Reflect on the types of tasks that are currently a priority for your team. Use the following figure to plot your team's top three priorities and where they fall on the spectrum from independence (that is, able to be completed independently) to interdependence (that is, more likely to build collective efficacy).

Top Priorities	Interdependence Level
Priority 1	Independent ———— Interdependent
Priority 2	Independent ———— Interdependent
Priority 3	Independent ———— Interdependent

Now take a moment to reflect. How many of your team's tasks were categorized as interdependent? Write them in the space provided.

Chapter 11

Consensus Over Ambiguity

By *building consensus*, school leaders can overcome *ambiguity* as an enemy of efficacy.

In this chapter, we examine how ambiguity becomes an enemy of efficacy. School leaders can overcome ambiguity by building consensus. Three key micro-moves leaders can rely on include guiding an affinity-mapping process, using the realm of concern and the realm of influence, and analyzing student work samples. School leaders achieve collective impact as they build consensus to overcome ambiguity.

Ambiguity as an Enemy of Efficacy

When something is ambiguous, it is open to multiple interpretations and therefore causes confusion and stifles progress. We have seen different types of ambiguity play out in schools and witnessed its destructive nature. Ambiguous roles, lack of consensus on priorities and goals, and ambiguity regarding teachers' collective efficacy to increase student achievement are a few examples.

First, consider the negative consequences that occur in schools where roles are ambiguous. In schools where teacher leadership is promoted, if there is a lack of agreement or clarity on the accompanying roles and responsibilities, teacher leaders will feel disempowered. Research demonstrates that role ambiguity is linked to decreased performance for vice principals (Çelik, 2013), increased levels of stress in school counselors (Culbreth, Scarborough, Banks-Johnson, & Solomon, 2005), and burnout for school athletic coaches (Capel, Sisley, & Desertrain, 2009). Furthermore, research shows that role ambiguity is a significant predictor of teacher efficacy (Macovei, Bumbuc, & Martinescu-Bădălan, 2023): the greater ambiguity regarding their role, the less efficacious educators will be. Therefore, ambiguity is an enemy of efficacy.

The *ambiguity effect*, first described by Daniel Ellsberg in 1961, is a cognitive bias where decision making is affected by a lack of information, or ambiguity.

Another example where ambiguity exists in schools is goals. In our experience, most teachers have difficulty completing the sentence, "An important improvement goal we are working on at our school is ______________." They are unsure of the school goals and often do not have clearly defined and agreed-on team goals. Furthermore, educators often have different interpretations of what a goal really is and face ambiguity about the terms, goals, priorities, and objectives. George Bradt (2023) defines *objectives* as "what needs to get done now—often quantified as goals" and *priorities* as "the few most important things that will deliver the objectives." Bradt (2023) states that priorities "spell out the how."

Finally, there is ambiguity regarding collective teacher efficacy in schools. In many conversations we've had with principals, leaders, and teachers, they've identified that they're working on collective efficacy but can't exactly pinpoint what it is that they're working on. The misguided notion of putting teams of teachers together and disguising collaboration as collective efficacy oversimplifies the complex nature of the construct. Cultivating collective efficacy isn't as simple as running collaborative team meetings, networking with other schools, and forming professional learning communities. Those things are ideal starting points, but collective efficacy is deeper than that. It's grown from the implementation of a clear, well-structured and executed strategy, built on the key sources and enabling conditions. Ultimately, it's formed around the collective belief that all students can realize their potential.

Researchers Terri Barber Kurz and Stephanie L. Knight (2004) find that collective efficacy is highly correlated with goal consensus and vision in schools.

We have also seen numerous social media posts depicting team-building challenges or activities designed to foster trust accompanied by phrases such as, "What a great way to build collective efficacy" or "#collective_efficacy alive and well @Anywhere Public School." Social media posts such as these oversimplify the complex nature of collective efficacy. However, when principals demonstrate the discipline to gain deeper understandings of fostering collective efficacy, it can make a huge difference in their schools.

To realize systemic and sustainable improvements in schools, principals can ensure that collective efficacy moves beyond just a catchphrase. Clear thinking must be invested in determining strategic ways to build consensus around major decisions. Collective impact is difficult to achieve if the team is not clear on what it is they're meant to be achieving in the first place. It's in these environments where consensus is built that leads to learning and growth. System and school leaders can take intentional steps to build consensus and overcome ambiguity as an enemy of efficacy.

Overcome Ambiguity by Building Consensus

School principals can overcome ambiguity through consensus building. Efficacy is built on mastery and vicarious experiences of strategies that have achieved success. Defining success, through clarity and consensus building, is a key move in knowing what to build toward. Teams need an agreed-on vision, codesigned goals, a select few priorities, and evidence-based strategies selected on students' needs.

Consensus building is the process of gathering input from stakeholders and reaching agreements as an important step in the decision-making process. It is important that principals seek consensus on major decisions (for example, vision, goals, priorities, school-improvement strategies) and put a process in place for reaching consensus. Consensus building reduces conflict, increases commitment, and leads to better solutions and greater buy-in.

Achieving consensus does not mean gaining unanimous agreement. Instead, it emphasizes a process of sharing ideas and exploring perspectives. When decisions are made based on consensus, they do not require unanimous consent. It's about reaching a place where those who disagree can still live with the decision. This allows acknowledging that the plan might not be perfect for everyone but it's acceptable enough to allow the team to move forward. Also, a non-negotiable is that all decisions are made in the best interest of students. Principals retain the ability to block a decision from proceeding if they believe that it could cause harm to students or the school community.

There are different models of consensus-building processes. Common to most are the following steps (Hanover Research, 2022; Madden, 2017).

1. Frame the problem—introduce and clarify the issue.
2. Generate open discussion.
3. Explore solutions by determining a set of viable consensus options.
4. Form and present a proposal.

5. Revise the proposal based on feedback.
6. Plan and execute the decision.

Three micro-moves leaders can use during the consensus-building process include (1) guiding an affinity-mapping process, (2) using the realm of concern versus the realm of influence protocol, and (3) analyzing student work samples.

"When leaders recognize the efficacy of their faculty is not strong, they might consider being more deliberate about modeling successful practice and working to build a positive culture for learning. It would be important to focus on a common mission for the school and work with staff to build consensus to the school improvement initiatives" (Prelli, 2016, p. 177).

Guiding an Affinity-Mapping Process

Affinity mapping is a collaborative process used to organize and make sense of information, ideas, and insights. Affinity mapping can be used to gain consensus among participants because it helps teachers find common ground and develop a shared understanding of the issues at hand. It involves gathering ideas, often on sticky notes, and then grouping similar items together based on their natural relationships or themes. Table 11.1 (page 167) illustrates various ideas for principals to lead teachers in affinity mapping.

Principals can lead the affinity-mapping process using the following steps.

1. **Brainstorming:** Teachers individually write down their ideas, observations, or data points on sticky notes, one idea per note.
2. **Sharing:** Teachers take turns silently sharing their ideas by placing their sticky notes on a wall or large table, without discussing or grouping them at this stage.
3. **Grouping:** Once all the ideas are shared, teachers work together to silently arrange the sticky notes into groups based on their natural affinities or relationships. Notes that seem related should be placed closer together.
4. **Naming:** After the grouping is complete, teachers discuss and agree on a name or label for each group, summarizing the common theme or idea that connects the items within the group.
5. **Discussing:** Principals then lead teachers in a discussion about the groups, their relationships, and any insights or conclusions they draw from the organized data.

Table 11.1: Uses for Affinity Mapping

Purpose	Use
Analyze student data	Teachers can use affinity mapping to group and analyze student performance data, identifying patterns, strengths, and areas for improvement.
Plan curriculum	When planning a new unit or curriculum, teachers can brainstorm ideas, resources, and activities, then use affinity mapping to organize these elements into coherent themes or learning objectives.
Solve problems	If teachers are facing a common challenge, such as student behavior issues or low engagement, principals can lead an affinity-mapping process to help them brainstorm potential solutions, group ideas into categories, and prioritize action steps.
Reflect on practices	Teachers can use affinity mapping to reflect on their teaching practices by grouping strategies, activities, or approaches that have been successful or identifying areas for professional growth and collaboration.
Develop schoolwide initiatives	When working on schoolwide initiatives, such as improving school culture or implementing new technology, teachers can use affinity mapping to gather input from various stakeholders, organize ideas, and develop action plans.

Tapping Into the Sources of Efficacy

By sharing ideas, grouping them based on relationships, and discussing insights, teachers gain exposure to each other's perspectives and experiences, building a shared understanding that contributes to collective efficacy.

By guiding an affinity-mapping process, principals can lead teachers in collaboratively making sense of complex information, identifying patterns and relationships, and developing a shared understanding of the issues and potential solutions. By ensuring that all participants have an equal opportunity to contribute their ideas during the brainstorming phase, affinity mapping helps ensure that all perspectives are considered. This inclusivity lays the foundation for consensus building. The silent grouping phase of affinity mapping allows teachers to organize ideas based on their natural affinities without the influence of more vocal team members. This step helps reduce the impact of power dynamics and encourages all participants to engage with the ideas on their own terms. When teachers work together to name the groups of ideas, they engage in a process of finding common themes and language to describe the issues at hand. This collaboration helps build shared understanding and consensus around the key topics. Principals can guide the process, ensuring that all voices are heard and that teachers remain focused on finding common ground and achieving consensus.

Using the Realm of Concern and Realm of Influence Protocol

The realm of concern and realm of influence protocol is a tool that helps teachers and teams identify and focus on areas where they have the power to make a difference. A principal can lead teachers in using this protocol to reach consensus using the following steps (National School Reform Faculty, n.d.b).

1. **Introduce the protocol:** The principal explains the concept of the realm of concern (things we care about but have limited control over) and the realm of influence (things we can directly impact or change).
2. **Identify concerns:** Ask teachers to brainstorm and list their concerns related to a specific issue or challenge. Encourage them to think broadly and include all relevant concerns.
3. **Categorize concerns:** Have teachers work together to categorize each concern as either within their realm of influence or realm of concern. See the "Planning for Action to Overcome Ambiguity" (page 172) reproducible at the end of this chapter.
4. **Focus on the realm of influence:** Guide teachers to focus their attention on the concerns that fall within their realm of influence. These are the areas where they have the power to make a difference.
5. **Brainstorm actions:** Encourage teachers to brainstorm specific actions they can take to address the concerns within their realm of influence. This step helps shift the focus from problems to solutions.
6. **Prioritize actions:** Have teachers work together to prioritize the brainstormed actions based on their potential impact and feasibility. This step helps build consensus around the most effective course of action.
7. **Develop an action plan:** Guide teachers in developing a concrete action plan based on the prioritized actions. Assign responsibilities, set timelines, and establish measures of success.
8. **Reflect and adjust:** Regularly review progress with teachers and make adjustments to the action plan as needed. Celebrate successes and learn from challenges.

By leading teachers through this protocol, the principal helps them focus their energy on areas where they have the power to make a difference. The collaborative process of categorizing concerns, brainstorming actions, and prioritizing solutions helps build consensus and ownership within the team. The principal's role is to facilitate the process, ensure all voices are heard, and guide the team toward a shared vision and action plan. By empowering teachers to focus on their realm of influence, the principal helps foster a sense of collective efficacy in addressing challenges and improving student outcomes.

Analyzing Student Work Samples

Consensus building is all about developing a shared understanding. One of the most powerful ways of generating consensus is with student work samples at the table. The power in this micro-move is using actual pieces of evidence in a way that stimulates conversation, questions, ideas, and debate, with the ultimate goal of reaching consensus.

Using a hypothetical example, during a planning meeting in preparation for an upcoming unit of work, a fourth-grade team bought a piece of work completed by a student from the previous year. In this instance, students were required to create a multimodal persuasive text to suit a particular purpose and audience. To be successful, students needed to demonstrate how authors used language features to persuade and build an argument.

Using an actual work sample completed at the grade-level standard from the previous year, the teaching team unpacked the artifact through an appreciative inquiry lens where they pose questions about students' strengths. Team members highlighted the strengths of the work and discussed what they anticipated their current cohort of students might find challenging. Going deeper, they strategized adjustments to their teaching sequence to ensure their current students would have multiple opportunities for success. Anticipating the challenge of ensuring all students had the opportunity to reach their goals, the team identified positive and proactive teaching strategies they felt would be helpful. The open dialogue during the meeting provided the team with an opportunity to clarify any misconceptions. During the meeting, even the most novice teacher had the confidence to speak up and share her concerns about a student in her class whom she felt may have difficulties. The group then shared ideas and strategies that she could try and test. The team mapped out their next steps for their teaching cycle.

Finally, the team leader checked in with each participant to ensure there was no ambiguity. This was done by simply asking, "Are we all good to go?" The team agreed to meet informally the following week to make sure they all got off to a good start and then tracked their progress over the four-week teaching cycle.

Tapping Into the Sources of Efficacy

As teachers examine real examples of student work together, they gain insights into each other's teaching practices, identify strengths and challenges, and share strategies for improvement, building a shared understanding and commitment to action based on collective expertise.

Building consensus is all about developing a shared understanding, followed by a shared commitment and then finally shared action. This micro-move is as simple as bringing student work to the table and then opening the dialogue to build consensus. The power of this approach is grounded in actual evidence of improving student work—something that all teachers become passionate about discussing.

Collective Impact

When school leaders successfully build consensus and overcome the detrimental effects of ambiguity, they create an environment where collective efficacy can thrive. By guiding affinity-mapping processes, using the realms of concern and influence protocol, and analyzing student work samples, principals can cultivate a culture of shared understanding, commitment, and action. By consistently engaging teachers in consensus-building activities, effective efficacy builders will foster a sense of ownership and collective responsibility among their staff, as they recognize the importance of their individual and collective efforts in driving school improvement. Consensus is important to realize collective impact. When school leaders embrace their role as a facilitator of consensus building, schools become places where ambiguity is replaced by shared understanding, a commitment to collaborative action, and an unwavering belief in the power of collective efficacy to transform student lives.

Ambiguity is an enemy of efficacy because when something is ambiguous teachers interpret things in different ways and that causes uncertainty and stifles progress. Ambiguity in roles, priorities, goals, and the understanding of collective teacher efficacy can lead to confusion, decreased performance, stress, and burnout among educators. Effective efficacy builders can overcome ambiguity by engaging teachers in consensus-building processes. Consensus building helps reduce conflict, increases commitment, and leads to better solutions and greater buy-in. It doesn't require unanimous agreement but aims to reach a place where everyone can accept the decision. Leaders can use micro-moves like affinity-mapping, the realms of concern and influence protocol, and analyzing student work to build consensus. Generating cohesive strategies and reaching consensus on learning priorities, through open dialogue and clear communication, can help schools achieve collective impact and overcome the negative effects of ambiguity on efficacy. Use the exercises and prompts in the reproducible "Planning for Action to Overcome Ambiguity" (page 172) to create effective consensus-building processes.

Planning for Action to Overcome Ambiguity

Use the following exercises to engage with the micro-moves discussed in chapter 11.

Affinity Mapping

Use the following steps to guide you through the process of affinity mapping. Introduce the purpose of affinity mapping (for example, analyzing student work, planning curriculum, solving problems, and so on) to set the context. Then follow these steps.

1. **Brainstorming:** Ask teachers to individually write down their ideas, observations, or data points on sticky notes, one idea per note.
2. **Sharing:** Lead teachers in taking turns placing their sticky notes on a wall or large table, without discussing or grouping them at this stage.
3. **Grouping:** Once all the ideas are shared, facilitate teachers in working together to silently arrange the sticky notes into groups based on their natural affinities or relationships. Notes that seem related should be placed closer together.
4. **Naming:** After the grouping is complete, ask teachers to discuss and agree on a name or label for each group and summarize the common theme or idea that connects the items within the group.
5. **Discussing:** Lead teachers in a discussion about the groups, their relationships, and any insights or conclusions they draw from the organized data.

By following this step-by-step process, teams can effectively use affinity mapping to organize large amounts of information, identify patterns and relationships, and gain a shared understanding of complex issues or challenges.

Realms of Concern and Influence

The purpose of this activity is to determine team members' concerns and which of those concerns the team has direct influence over. This will help identify student learning needs, narrow down a goal, and build consensus.

To begin, draw three concentric circles of increasing size on a flip chart as shown in the following figure.

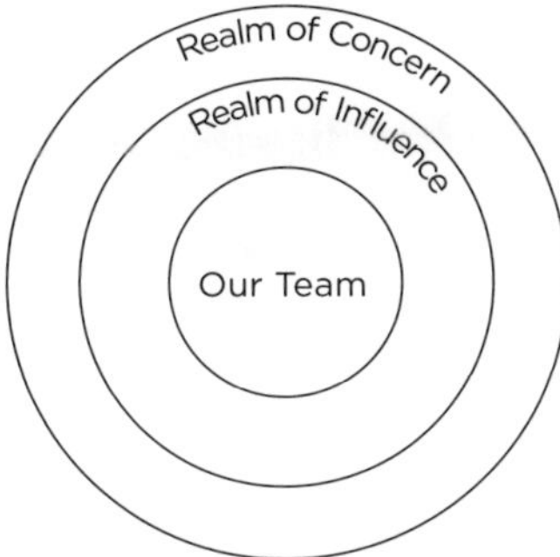

Source: Adapted from National School Reform Faculty, n.d.

Use the following instructions to guide the activity (National School Reform Faculty, n.d.).

1. The team visualizes themselves in the central circle.
2. Ask team members to list student learning needs, writing each need on an individual sticky note. Encourage them to list *everything* they can think of related to their students' learning needs. Once the brainstorming is complete, ask the team to place the sticky notes on the outer ring. These ideas represent the realm of concern.
3. Next, ask the team to determine which issues from the outer ring they have influence over. Ask them to move the sticky notes naming such issues into the inner circle (realms of influence). Encourage them to think critically about what they place in the realm of influence.

Note that as the team works to change their realm of influence, their realm of influence gets larger and they will begin to have more influence to effect change in their realm of concern.

Consider the following questions for discussion (National School Reform Faculty, n.d.).

1. What do you notice? What stands out? What is significant to you?
2. What is the difference between the *realm of concern* list and the *realm of influence* list?
3. What does this mean for our work?
4. What goals will your team work toward?

Analyzing Student Work Samples

Reflect on the processes in your context to moderate and analyze student work samples with a view to building consensus and developing a shared understanding.

Who is around the table when the team analyzes student work samples?

What questions is the team aiming to explore?

How does the team reach consensus on the path forward?

What commitment to action does the team make?

Reference

National School Reform Faculty. (n.d.). *Realms of concern and influence*. Accessed at www.nsrfharmony.org/wp-content/uploads/2017/10/realms_concern_influence_0.pdf on September 3, 2024.

Chapter 12

Focus Over Fragmentation

By *focusing on implementation*, school leaders can overcome *fragmentation* as an enemy of efficacy.

In this chapter, we explore how fragmentation becomes an enemy of efficacy. School leaders can overcome fragmentation by focusing on implementation. Three key micro-moves leaders can use include gatekeeping, applying the 80/20 principle, and prioritizing evidence-based strategies. School leaders achieve collective impact as they focus on implementation and overcome fragmentation.

Fragmentation as an Enemy of Efficacy

Through our careers, we've lost count of the initiatives, either school or system led, that have lost traction, failed to fire, or just simply disappeared. Principals know that schools are often seen as the perfect testing grounds for a range of programs and initiatives, some of which are very short lived. The problem with reform agendas placed on schools, unrelated to the core business of delivering high-impact teaching and learning, is that they take the focus away from instructional leadership efforts and minimize the opportunity to foster collective efficacy. This fragmentation results in lost opportunities and a sense of confusion. Michael Fullan and Joanne Quinn (2016) wisely pose the question, "How do you turn overload and fragmentation into focus and coherence?" (p. ix). This highlights how, in many situations, constant overload, disconnect, and fragmentation can overwhelm the moral purpose of even the most resilient team.

Fragmentation is the lack of integration, coordination, and collaboration that occurs within and across schools, educational organizations, and systems. In their urgency to get things done, school faculty will often lock themselves into narrowly defined courses of action. Some school systems make the mistake of pursuing too-good-to-be-true initiatives, grasping at silver bullets or working in silos, often seeking implementation by way of compliance. The all-too-common result is that well-intended initiatives end up creating conflict for practitioners and those who the initiative was intended to serve. Often, different initiatives within schools may clash with one another, producing disappointing results. Disappointing results then lead reformers to abandon their strategy and try something new, but without changing how they work to implement it. This creates an ongoing cycle, failing to produce the momentum needed to boost collective efficacy.

Timperley and Robinson (2000) further suggest that the problem of workload is compounded by the norm of collegiality, which precludes public criticism of practices that are privately judged inadequate. In the task force, the supportive and inclusive attributes of collegiality prevented evaluations of current initiatives or the exercise of mutual accountability.

Researchers Helen Timperley and Viviane Robinson (2000) document a familiar example of this in a case study that examines the workload and professional culture of teachers. Teachers representing various departments in a high school were recruited to a task force on improving the achievement of minority students. Over a period of three to four years, the number of programs and initiatives to assist minority students increased from three to thirteen. During this period, no programs were discontinued or evaluated for their effectiveness; more were simply added on to those already in place. As year four drew to a close, the task force had accomplished little.

Timperley and Robinson (2000) locate the challenge for school principals in facilitating the realization of potential benefits without increasing teachers' workloads to unacceptable levels. In this case study, both the principal and the senior management knew of the existing initiatives and had reservations about the effectiveness and expense of some of them. School leaders inadvertently created conditions that allowed the task force to continue with ineffective processes. This is an example of how a lack of integration, coordination, and collaboration caused fragmentation in a school.

To highlight the issue of fragmentation, Anthony S. Bryk, John Q. Easton, David Kerbow, Sharon G. Rollow, and Penny Bender Sebring (1993) coined the term *Christmas tree schools* (p. 14) to describe what was happening to a number of Chicago schools in the city's reform efforts. These schools had adopted a jumble of disconnected programs with largely superficial implementation. As a result, what looked good, new, and shiny didn't actually amount to much by way of impact. Bryk and colleagues write, "the branches of the Christmas tree school may glitter with new ornaments while the trunk of the tree—the vitality of the school's core program—may largely go unattended" (p. 14). Schools seeking the next shiny ornament to add to their improvement strategy can inadvertently add a layer of fragmentation and have an inverse effect on improvement efforts.

To realize systemic and sustainable improvements in schools, principals can ensure that teams reduce fragmentation and instead focus on elevating what is essential to improve student outcomes. School leaders can maintain a focus to ensure that evidence-based practices are truly implemented. System and school leaders can take intentional steps to increase focus and overcome fragmentation as an enemy of efficacy.

Fullan and Quinn (2016) write, "While professional learning materials, workshops, presenters, and programs abound, we often see a fragmented approach, focused on fixing individuals. Current programs solicit participation from individual schools and educators and often do not include systematic and sustained follow up. The result is an overwhelming range of solutions without coherence of sustainability" (p. 57).

Overcome Fragmentation With Implementation

School principals can provide the clear and focused leadership required to fix school- and system-level fragmentation. Author and former teacher Mike Schmoker (2011) notes that the failure to improve schools isn't because the knowledge of how to do so doesn't exist. Schmoker (2011) suggests that it's "our failure to be clear and focused" (p. 13) in supporting the implementation of a few key priorities that is the problem. He argues, "We will never master or implement what is most important for kids if we continue to pursue multiple new initiatives *before* we implement our highest priority strategies and structures" (Schmoker, 2011, p. 15). School leaders can focus on key priorities and implementation to overcome fragmentation as an enemy of efficacy.

Research shows that in schools where collective efficacy is established, teachers are more likely to reach deeper levels of implementation (Cantrell & Callaway, 2008; Parks, Solmon, & Lee, 2007; Tschannen-Moran, 2001). In one example, education researchers Susan Chambers Cantrell and Patricia Callaway (2008) examine the collective efficacy beliefs of junior high school teachers whose implementation patterns differed based on a yearlong professional development program. The program aimed to integrate literacy strategies into content area classrooms. The researchers found that teachers who exhibited higher levels of collective efficacy required less time to internalize literacy strategies and determine how to use them to teach content, were more successful in working through the barriers they encountered (including time constraints), and showed greater persistence in "finding resources for multiple strategies and approaches to meeting the needs of students" (p. 1746). Fostering efficacy will help in attaining deeper levels of implementation.

In a meta-analysis of sixty-nine studies, Robert J. Marzano, Timothy Waters, and Brian A. McNulty (2005) identify twenty-one leadership behaviors that had a significant effect on student achievement. A prime example of these identified leadership responsibilities, one highly relevant for treating system-level fragmentation, is *focus*. System and school leaders can take intentional steps to overcome fragmentation as an enemy of efficacy and maintain focus on the implementation of evidence-based practices by employing three micro-moves outlined in this chapter. These three micro-moves include (1) gatekeeping, (2) applying the 80/20 principle, and (3) prioritizing evidence-based strategies.

Gatekeeping

After a series of underwhelming results in previous competitions and not having won a gold medal in over a century, the British rowing team took a focused approach into their preparations for the 2000 Sydney Olympic Games. They developed a useful, yet remarkably simple, strategy that was a game changer for their performance.

With a totally focused approach, they developed a one-question prompt for every decision they made. This question was their guiding light and helped to provide a measure for every situation, decision, or circumstance. When presented with a decision, a challenge, or an opportunity, every member of the team committed to asking themselves that one key question: "Will it make the boat go faster?"

Asked to attend a late-night party the night before a training session? The response: "Will it make the boat go faster?" If the answer was no, then the decision was no. Tempted to eat that extra slice of pizza? The response: "Will it make the boat go faster?" Again, if the answer was no, then the decision was no. This yardstick to assist in their decision making ultimately propelled the British team to Olympic glory as they blitzed their competition. The secret to their performance was focus. By clearing the confusion caused by competing priorities or disconnected strategies, the team developed crystal-clear thinking around one goal. The team demonstrated that they were the gatekeepers, protecting their priorities from any chance of fragmentation. If it did not assist the ultimate goal, it wasn't allowed through the gate.

Principals can practice focus over fragmentation by controlling what gets through the gate in their schools. While the rowing team was focused on making the boat go faster, school teams' overall focus is improving student outcomes. Of course, schools are unique, and most schools have identified more precise priorities based on student learning needs, such as improving students' ability to self-regulate, their reading comprehension, or their problem-solving skills, to name a few. Like the other micro-moves described in this book, practicing the micro-move of gatekeeping is fairly simple. After identifying one or two priorities, as educators consider any and every new idea, initiative, or program, they constantly ask the question, "Will it improve students' [insert priority here]?" If the answer is no, don't let it through the gate.

Tapping Into the Sources of Efficacy

When educators consistently ask themselves and each other whether a decision or action will directly contribute to improving a specific student outcome, they collectively witness the impact of their aligned and purposeful choices, reinforcing their belief in the team's ability to make a difference.

Applying the 80/20 Principle

Executive director of National Staff Development Council Dennis Sparks (2007) offers strategies for improving student outcomes in his book *Leading for Results*. One strategy particularly applicable to focusing on implementation over fragmentation is the 80/20 principle, which states that 80 percent of outcomes result from 20 percent of causes. In other words, a minority of causes, inputs, or effort usually lead to a majority of the results, outcomes, or rewards. This is also known as the Pareto principle, named after Vilfredo Pareto, the economist who first wrote about the 80/20 connection in 1906. This brings us back to the idea of cause-and-effect relationships that we discussed in chapter 1 (page 13). What are some of the things in the school that are producing (causing) a disproportionate share of the results (effect) the faculty values the most?

Sparks (2007) states, "some things we do as leaders make an important contribution to the achievement of our goals. Other things we do make little difference"

(p. 25). He also points out the "ability to discriminate between these two categories of things and to focus our efforts on the former category is essential in producing results and in achieving those results more efficiently" (p. 25). Principals can apply the 80/20 principle and identify the 20 percent of things in the school that are likely causing 80 percent of the outcomes and then determine how to reduce or eliminate the actions and activities that are not having an impact. Educational leaders Simon Breakspear and Michael Rosenbrock (2024) refer to this as the pruning principle. Arran Hamilton, John Hattie, and Dylan Wiliam (2023) and Peter M. DeWitt (2022) refer to this as *de-implementation.*

Hamilton and colleagues (2023) state, "everyone needs to know that it's OK to (collectively) do less to achieve more" (p. 67). They even suggest that "it might even be perfectly OK to do less to achieve the same" (p. 67). In our experience, teachers would welcome this idea as many feel overworked, overloaded, and constantly pressed for time. In applying the 80/20 principle, school leaders should do the following.

- Collect and review evidence on various aspects of the school operations and corelate it with student-performance measures.
- Determine which activities, strategies, or initiatives are contributing to improvements in student learning (for example, specific teaching strategies, professional learning, student support services, curriculum, school policies and procedures, and so on).
- Decide how to allocate more effort, time, and resources to these areas.
- Reduce low-impact activities.
- Monitor the effectiveness of changes and make adjustments accordingly.
- Be sure to involve staff and communicate the rationale and results as you engage in this process of de-implementation.

However, even though teachers would welcome things being taken off their plate, sometimes they find it hard to let go of outdated or ineffective practices for a variety of reasons.

- "But this is the way we've always done it around here."
- "I swear by this strategy."
- "I enjoy this unit!"

Because of this, Hamilton and colleagues (2023) suggest that it's beneficial for leaders to identify things that might derail de-implementation and then create a plan to mitigate them.

Tapping Into the Sources of Efficacy

Applying the 80/20 principle can lead to vicarious experiences that contribute to collective efficacy by focusing the team's efforts on the most impactful practices. As educators collectively identify and prioritize the 20 percent of actions that yield 80 percent of the desired results, they witness the significant impact of their focused efforts, reinforcing their belief in the team's ability to make a difference through strategic choices.

The 80/20 principle is about helping to identify and focus only on the things that will deeply enhance student outcomes. By removing many of the things that are not producing results to make room to focus on the things that matter more, principals will signal that the selected strategies aren't going away and that everyone is expected to do their part.

Prioritizing Evidence-Based Strategies

Principals can guide teachers to focus on practices shown to have a positive impact on student outcomes. Jenni Donohoo and Steven Katz (2020) point out that "we are on fairly solid ground when it comes to the *what* of school improvement" (p. 4) and that it's the "quality implementation of evidence-based strategies that remains a consistent and widespread challenge when it comes to school improvement efforts" (p. 5). Educators do not need any further research on what's supposed to work in schools. To ensure that evidence-based practices are truly and efficiently implemented, principals must make constant efforts to prioritize their use in classrooms.

In fact, measurable gains in student achievement cannot be realized until schools reach deep levels of implementation. Reeves's (2008) research demonstrates that 90 percent or more of the faculty adopting initiatives is the threshold if we want to see changes resulting in measurable outcomes for students. However, when teachers first try new strategies in their classrooms, they've had little practice using them and may not implement them with fidelity. And, of course, the effectiveness of the strategy is dependent on how it's used.

Tapping Into the Sources of Efficacy

When principals guide teachers to focus on implementing proven practices with fidelity and engage them in reviewing their progress, educators witness the positive impact of these strategies on student outcomes. This shared experience of success reinforces the team's belief in their collective ability to make a difference through the consistent use of effective practices.

Robert J. Marzano (2012, 2017) points out that the effect sizes of various instructional strategies vary from one study to another and provides an example from his own research. When studying the impact of identifying differences and similarities as a strategy, Marzano (2012) finds that in one study it was associated with a 45 percentile gain but in a different study only an 18 percentile gain. He attributes the difference in impact to different levels of use and notes that "how a teacher uses a strategy is key to how effective the strategy is" (Marzano, 2012, p. 88). He shares four levels of implementation (from beginning to developing to applying to innovating) and observes that when educators first use a strategy, they aren't very fluent with it and therefore are prone to errors. He attributes the difference in reported effect sizes to the fact that teachers gain proficiency the more they execute and practice it. Therefore, it's important for principals to reinforce the use of evidence-based strategies in classrooms.

Megan Tschannen-Moran (2001) reports that implementation of a conflict management program, infused via curriculum integration, was positively related to collective teacher efficacy in a study involving fifty high schools in the United States.

Principals can do so by concentrating publicly and persistently on improving the quality of classroom instruction. School leaders can engage teachers and teams in reviewing their fidelity of using the strategies and use this information to determine what further implementation supports teachers need. Ideas for doing so include the following.

- Identify what fidelity looks like for each strategy.
- Ask teachers to evaluate their own level of implementation.
- Organize peer observations focused on strategy implementation.
- Look for and share patterns and trends in implementation throughout the school.
- Lead collaborative conversations in which teachers identify implementation barriers and brainstorm solutions.
- Regularly solicit input from teachers on the implementation support they need and the effectiveness of various supports so you can adjust approaches as needed.

By focusing on prioritizing evidence-based practices, principals can overcome fragmentation and realize greater outcomes for students.

Collective Impact

When school leaders successfully focus on implementation and overcome the detrimental effects of fragmentation, they create an environment where collective efficacy can thrive. By practicing effective gatekeeping, applying the 80/20 principle, and prioritizing evidence-based strategies, principals can cultivate a culture of clarity, efficiency, and continuous improvement. School leaders have the power to maintain a laser-like focus on the initiatives and practices that yield the greatest impact on student outcomes while eliminating those that do not contribute to the school's core mission. By consistently communicating the importance of focused effort and providing the necessary support for deep implementation, effective efficacy builders will foster a sense of shared purpose and collective responsibility among their staff. Collective impact requires a commitment to focus. When school leaders focus their efforts on implementation, fragmentation is replaced by a shared sense of direction, a willingness to prioritize what matters most, and an unwavering belief in the power of collective efficacy to drive transformative change for all learners.

Fragmentation is an enemy of efficacy because it is a distracting factor for schools. Educators looking for the next shiny thing to add to their repertoire can inadvertently lose focus on their core business. Effective efficacy builders can overcome fragmentation by ensuring that they only let new ideas and programs related to their priorities and with the potential to improve student outcomes through the gate. A focused approach amplifies the impact of evidence-based strategies and reduces the likelihood of an ad hoc change in direction causing the murkiness of a fragmented approach. A focused approach requires judicious and persistent leadership. School leaders can also reduce activities that are not yielding improved results. Finally, school leaders can make constant efforts to prioritize evidence-based strategies. Use the exercises and prompts in the reproducible "Planning for Action to Overcome Fragmentation" (page 184) to practice focusing on implementation.

Planning for Action to Overcome Fragmentation

Use the following exercises to engage with the micro-moves discussed in chapter 12.

Gatekeeping

In the following figure, list your guiding question. (For example, will this expand students' vocabulary in writing?) Then collectively brainstorm with your team on the following questions: What is able to pass through your gates? What needs more thinking? What will not pass?

Guiding question: ______________________________?		
Able to pass through the gates	Need to think more about	Does not pass through the gates

Applying the 80/20 Principle

List activities happening at your school that you believe produce results (that is, the 20 percent of things that produce 80 percent of the results).

List things that you could diminish or eliminate (that is, the 80 percent of things that produce only 20 percent of the results).

What are some things that might derail de-implementation?

How might you mitigate these things?

Prioritizing Evidence-Based Strategies

In the space provided, outline the strategy that you plan on implementing as part of your improvement agenda. Next, do some research with your team members to find the evidence base to support your strategy.

For example, if you've chosen to improve the quality of written feedback to students, your team might source evidence-proven strategies and research where those strategies have been successful.

Epilogue

Many of the challenges educators face in schools center on complex problems that require them to work together with a collective voice to change students' lives for the better. The strength of teachers and leaders rests largely in their sense of collective efficacy that they can solve the problems they face to improve learning and well-being outcomes through collective impact. You now know that *collective impact* is the impact achieved through high levels of collective efficacy. This book provides the blueprint to achieve collective success and realize impact greater than any individual effort could accomplish.

This book started with two aims. The first was to build further awareness of collective efficacy—what it is and why it matters. The second aim was to help bridge the gap between theory and practice. In achieving the first aim, each of the four parts outlined the sources of collective efficacy, demonstrating how efficacy beliefs are formed, why they're important, and how they contribute to school and system improvement. This background information was designed to help you better understand the theoretical foundations on which we based our strategies for overcoming the enemies of efficacy.

The second aim of the book was to help bridge the gap between theory and practice. To achieve this, we presented twelve theories of actions for overcoming the enemies of efficacy. These theories include overarching leadership actions providing proven practices for driving meaningful improvement in schools. You then encountered the twelve enemies of efficacy, which can sabotage the pathway to achieving collective efficacy. By identifying potential enemies of efficacy, school and system leaders can increase their awareness of the barriers that prevent efficacy from developing.

You encountered three micro-moves to overcome each enemy. The micro-moves are those small steps educators can take to engage teachers and leaders meaningfully and respectfully in school improvement. Though small, these moves can have a large impact in generating the momentum and enthusiasm needed to realize collective efficacy and impact. The micro-moves you learned won't build efficacy alone. They also may not build efficacy quickly. Think of the micro-moves as the one percenters—the small things that make the big difference. These are the little things that, applied consistently and with fidelity, will ultimately build high levels of collective efficacy.

At the conclusion of each chapter, you engaged with a planning for action reproducible. We designed these exercises and prompts to provide practical strategies for action. These reproducibles include actions you can apply immediately—at the next faculty meeting, during a leadership meeting, or simply when principals are reflecting on how to improve their practice. We encourage you to look for opportunities to integrate the micro-moves into everyday practice and use the planning for action reproducibles as tools to assist. The appendix (page 193) includes a summary of the micro-moves linked to each theory of action. Consider printing this summary and placing it in a prominent location for easy reference.

One of the central purposes that inspired us to write this book was our goal of increasing levels of collective efficacy in all schools. Collective efficacy is not a new concept. While research dates back several decades (Bandura, 1977; Guskey, 1987), many educators are still unfamiliar with the concept of collective efficacy or unaware of the strength of the evidence that supports its impact. Furthermore, given its potential impact, school leaders continue to look for practical ways to instill and strengthen collective efficacy in their schools. Too often, schools across the globe offer excuses for their results. Our view was to flip that thinking and leverage the collective expertise of school teams to deliver *results over excuses*.

Let's take a look at some of the more macro-level considerations for fostering efficacy in schools. While the key feature in overcoming the enemies of efficacy is the small but mighty micro-moves, an efficacious leader will be aware of the macro-level considerations that enable the micro-moves to work most effectively.

Macro-Level Considerations

Marco-level considerations are the *big picture* preconditions necessary to foster collective efficacy. At the system level, these are the strategic considerations that create the environment for collective efficacy to flourish system wide. At the school level, macro-moves are the things school principals do to cultivate an environment where collective efficacy is created, maintained, and sustained, producing improved learning outcomes. In the following sections, we discuss three macro-level considerations: systems and structures, instructional leadership, and collective experimentation. In addition to the micro-moves shared in each chapter, an efficacious leader should understand these three macro-level considerations.

Systems and Structures

School structures designed to enable quality collaboration are a predominant feature of the research into building collective efficacy. Simply put, this refers to how easily educators are able to connect, collaborate, solve problems, and celebrate as part of their work. Goddard and colleagues (2017) state, "principals in schools with relatively high collective efficacy were often credited by teachers for putting structures in place that enabled teacher collaboration for instructional improvement" (p.13). Further, they report, "in contrast, we saw evidence of more autocratic leadership and limited evidence of productive collaboration in schools with relatively low levels of collective efficacy" (Goddard et al., 2017, p. 231).

Beauchamp and colleagues (2014) find, "Collaboration was an especially powerful tool contributing to teachers' collective efficacy and underscores the importance of building a sense of collective efficacy through whole-school collaborative activities" (p. 51).

Researchers John Ross, Anne Hogaboam-Gray, and Peter Gray (2004) examine the antecedents of collective teacher efficacy and determine that school processes have a strong influence on the collective efficacy of teachers. They share that school processes that contribute to a cohesive, supportive environment are likely to also contribute to each of the four sources of efficacy information, which are mastery experiences, vicarious experience, social persuasion, and affective states. For example, social interactions (among teachers and with administrators) influence whether teachers interpret prior achievement scores as evidence of mastery experiences. In relation to vicarious experiences, Ross and colleagues (2004) note that a "heightened interaction among teachers provided opportunities to observe the contribution of the collective to individual success . . . increasing perceptions of their individual and collective success and expectations for the future" (p. 167). When considering affective states, Ross and colleagues (2004) state, "social processes that generate peer support are likely to reduce the effects of negative emotions on collective teacher efficacy beliefs" (p. 167). The greater degree of purposeful collaboration, connected to instructional improvement, the greater the likelihood of cultivating collective efficacy. This macro-move sees leaders embedding school- and system-level structures to prioritize high-quality collaboration.

Tapping Into the Sources of Efficacy

By working together to solve problems, create resources, and build capability, teachers can experience success and develop a sense of collective accomplishment, which contribute to their collective efficacy.

Instructional Leadership

The second macro-level consideration is the link between collective efficacy and instructional leadership. Researchers Roger Goddard, Yvonne Goddard, Eun Sook Kim, and Robert Miller, (2015) were interested in finding out how leadership impacts what teachers do to become more effective. They argue that school environments are more productive when principals work collaboratively with teachers to develop collective expertise. Goddard and colleagues (2015) are specifically interested in the relationship between instructional leadership, teacher collaboration, and collective efficacy and how this relationship impacts student learning. In their study, they conclude the following.

- The principals' instructional leadership strongly predicts the degree to which teachers' collaborations focus on instructional improvement.
- Teachers' collaboration for instructional improvement is a strong direct predictor of collective efficacy.
- The principals' instructional leadership is a significant positive predictor of collective efficacy beliefs through its influence on teachers' collaborative work.
- Perceived collective efficacy is a significant positive predictor of differences among schools in student achievement (Goddard et al., 2015).

Goddard and colleagues (2015) indicate that the "more robust the sense of collective efficacy characterizing the schools in our sample, the greater their levels of student achievement, even after controlling for school and student background characteristics and prior levels of student achievement" (p. 525). Salloum (2021) supports this macro-level consideration by identifying instructional program coherence, "specifically how teachers work together and are supported in enacting the common instructional framework" (p. 234) to bolster sources of efficacy within the school.

We cite this research to highlight that school leaders who leverage opportunities for collaboration, specifically with an instructional intent, and provide teachers (or schools) with opportunities to learn with and from one another, can grow their levels of collective efficacy. The power of this macro-level move rests in creating the conditions to maximize the opportunity to work together to influence student learning outcomes.

Experimentation

The final macro-move is to promote and encourage a culture of experimentation. A sense of intellectual curiosity is sparked when teachers are given permission to experiment with instructional improvement strategies. The purpose of encouraging experimentation is to strengthen the sense of agency, display an openness to learning, and harvest and utilize staff knowledge, skills, and expertise to find solutions to persistent problems. One of the most effective pathways is through an inquiry stance. An *inquiry stance* describes educators working together in inquiry communities to ask questions, gain knowledge, and implement ideas into their practice.

Promoting an inquiry stance sees teachers become inquisitive, open minded, curious, and encouraging as they shape questions for exploration, such as "How could we better design a system of written feedback that achieves its desired impact?" or "How can we design unique strategies to increase the school attendance rates of our Indigenous students?" An inquiry stance allows teachers to explore the questions, trial strategies, and capture feedback. Taking an inquiry stance and promoting a culture of experimentation also reinforce a feeling of psychological safety (explored in chapter 6, page 76). As teams experiment and learn and grow from their reflections, collective efficacy grows. Experimentation is not just limited to solving existing problems; it can also be used to trial innovative new methods.

In many school districts in Ontario, Canada, teams of teachers engage in cycles of inquiry using a simple four-stage model of planning, acting, observing, and reflecting. Teachers determine an area of their practice they want to improve, or a student learning need they want to address, and then create a guiding question that will drive their inquiry, such as "How can we improve student engagement during class discussions?" Teachers collect relevant data to inform their inquiry, such as student work samples, observation notes, and feedback from colleagues. Teachers examine the evidence to identify patterns, insights, and areas for growth. Then, based on that analysis, teachers implement changes in their practice, such as trying new instructional strategies or resources. Teachers reflect on the effectiveness of their actions and make adjustments as needed, continuing the cycle of inquiry and improvement.

This inquiry cycle provides a structured approach to professional learning grounded in teachers' own practice and driven by their desire to improve student outcomes. By engaging in this ongoing process of planning, acting, observing, and reflecting, teachers can develop a deeper understanding of their craft and enhance their efficacy in their schools.

Finally, experimentation with artificial intelligence (AI) is a new frontier in the collective efficacy field. Educators should view leveraging the strength of AI as an efficacy partner and as an opportunity for further exploration. For schools to achieve collective impact, a wise strategy is to experiment with all available resources to develop that shared conviction that educators can use to make a difference.

A Final Note

The macro-level considerations we have described are low-cost, high-impact ways of creating the conditions to cultivate collective efficacy. Providing the platform for teachers to leverage their collective strength can lead to success in attaining positive outcomes. Fostering high-quality collaboration, developing instructional program coherence, and encouraging experimentation spark teachers' intellectual curiosity and give them the opportunity to collectively flourish. Doing so also strengthens their sense of agency and utilizes staff's knowledge, skills, and expertise to find solutions to persistent problems.

In conclusion, we define *collective impact* as the impact made possible through high levels of collective efficacy. This is the impact achieved when school and system leaders identify the enemies of efficacy within their context and use micro-moves to overcome them. This type of impact calls on efficacious leaders to mobilize the collective, thereby achieving an impact far more powerful than any individual working alone can accomplish. Collective impact is made possible by overcoming the enemies of efficacy.

Appendix

Summaries of the Micro-Moves

This appendix summarizes the thirty-six micro-moves we present in this book. This summary provides you with a quick reference and reminder of the moves and how to execute them. Visit go.SolutionTree.com/teacherefficacy for a free reproducible version of this appendix.

Feedback Over Blame (Chapter 1)

Through *effective feedback*, school leaders can overcome *blame* as an enemy of efficacy.

Normalizing Coaching Feedback

Coaching feedback is designed to support teachers in improving their instructional practices. Principals help reduce evaluation defensiveness when they separate coaching feedback from evaluative feedback. By delivering coaching feedback regularly, principals can normalize it and teachers will receive it as a supportive effort to help them improve.

Emphasizing the Role of Effort and Strategy Use

Principals focus on the things that teachers do that make a positive difference for students by emphasizing the role of strategy and effort. Providing attributional feedback that links student performance outcomes with teachers' efforts and selection of strategies helps to reduce the effects of the attribution bias.

Providing Frequent Updating

It's too late to wait for annual standardized test scores to determine impact. Principals regularly engaging teachers in processes that provide up-to-date information about students' progress and achievement helps create a sense of momentum and reinforces the belief that educators within the school are capable of overcoming challenges.

Perspective Over Magnitude (Chapter 2)

By *framing challenges appropriately*, school leaders can overcome *magnitude* as an enemy of efficacy.

Framing Through Emphasizing and De-Emphasizing

Leaders can help teachers perceive challenges as more manageable by framing them positively. This involves emphasizing available resources, past successes, teamwork, potential positive outcomes, and staff resilience. It also involves de-emphasizing complexity, uncertainty, time pressure, and factors beyond the school's control. By doing so, principals help to create a more empowering narrative that encourages a focus on actionable steps.

Framing Different Futures

Educators can disrupt students' probable futures, which are based on circumstances and societal expectations. By framing preferable futures, leaders inspire teachers to shape students' lives through high expectations. By challenging predetermined outcomes and designing learning experiences, teachers empower students to become change agents, breaking free from limitations and realizing their full potential.

Framing Challenges Into Smaller Pieces

Principals can help overwhelmed teachers by breaking challenges into manageable pieces. This involves identifying key components, developing a step-by-step plan, prioritizing pressing aspects, focusing on a few priorities at a time, scheduling regular check-ins to review progress and reassess, maintaining open communication, and being flexible in addressing emerging needs.

Commitment Over Compliance (Chapter 3)

By *garnering commitment*, school leaders can overcome *compliance* as an enemy of efficacy.

Highlighting a Gap

By presenting disaggregated data and highlighting a gap, principals help to create a discrepancy between how things currently are and how things could be. By sharing gaps in achievement between different groups of students, leaders create a demand to reduce the gap and garner greater commitment to achieving more equitable outcomes.

Learning From Marker Students

A *marker student* is a student who is not progressing as expected and the teacher is uncertain why. Principals work with teachers in learning about and supporting marker students. Leaders can help teachers analyze how marker students respond to different types of instruction, gain information regarding impact, and determine next steps.

Surfacing the Cost of Inaction

Helping teachers see the difference between their current and potential practices by emphasizing what they are losing by doing nothing raises awareness of the omission bias. The omission bias leads teachers to perceive potential harm from new actions as more negative than the harm caused by inaction. By emphasizing the negative consequences of inaction, principals can encourage teachers to try new approaches.

Positivity Over Negativity (Chapter 4)

By *elevating positivity*, school leaders can overcome *negativity* as an enemy of efficacy.

Labeling Emotions

As an ex-FBI hostage negotiator, Voss (2017) suggests using labeling to validate emotions and diffuse negative ones. To acknowledge feelings without confrontation, start with a neutral statement of understanding, such as "It seems like. . . ." Labeling negative emotions diminishes them, while labeling positive ones reinforces them. Remember, emotions are contagious.

Recognizing and Celebrating Progress

Instructional leadership teams and collaborative teams build collective efficacy by celebrating progress. Strategies include holding recognition circles, focusing on strengths and achievements, examining student work positively, and sharing success stories. These foster positive dialogue, counter negative narratives, support team members, enhance collective efficacy, promote well-being, and reduce stress and burnout.

Leveraging the Power of the Narrative

Engaging teachers to co-construct a compelling collective efficacy narrative is a powerful micro-move for elevating positivity in schools. This narrative shapes the school's culture, cultivates pride and belonging, and reinforces a strong sense of efficacy by empowering staff and students to share stories of overcoming obstacles. The narrative also reaffirms team efforts and crystallizes core values and practices.

Psychological Safety Over Judgment (Chapter 5)

By *enhancing psychological safety*, school leaders can overcome *judgment* as an enemy of efficacy.

Understanding Different Ways of Communicating

Understanding communication styles is crucial for building psychological safety within a team. Have members share preferences in three areas: communication style, working style, and deeper connections. Facilitators create a safe sharing environment by encouraging input and demonstrating vulnerability. Leaders can use the information to differentiate tasks, provide personalized feedback, establish protocols, and structure meetings accordingly.

Modeling the Norms of Collaboration

Establishing collaboration norms is crucial for effective teamwork. Three key norms are (1) inviting all voices to contribute, (2) suspending judgment and increasing curiosity when presented with new perspectives, and (3) responding productively by agreeing on next steps. Initially stated explicitly, these norms eventually become understood ways of working, fostering a culture of collaboration and psychological safety.

Sharing Feedback

Leaders can establish lasting psychological safety by sharing past feedback they've received rather than seeking new feedback. Sharing feedback normalizes vulnerability, builds trust, and encourages others to give actionable feedback over time. While initially uncomfortable, this practice helps leaders demonstrate openness to criticism, acknowledge limitations, and create an environment that sustains psychological safety.

Well-Being Over Uncertainty (Chapter 6)

By *prioritizing well-being*, school leaders can overcome *uncertainty* as an enemy of efficacy.

Building Workplace Well-Being Profiles

Principals can reduce uncertainty by creating workplace well-being profiles that assess teachers' engagement, productivity, and performance and growth. These profiles help principals understand teachers' experiences, reduce interpersonal mush, and identify areas for improvement. By using a Likert scale, teachers provide baseline data on their well-being, allowing principals to take action and address issues such as low engagement, productivity, or performance and growth scores.

Addressing Teachers' Concerns

Principals can reduce teachers' stress during change by addressing their Stages of Concern: unconcerned, informational, personal, management, consequence, collaboration, and refocusing. Aligning support with teachers' specific stage of concern, such as providing information, encouragement, or vicarious learning opportunities, can build clarity and efficacy. Listening to concerns and offering appropriate support foster well-being and effective coping with change.

Increasing Interpersonal Clarity

Principals can increase interpersonal clarity and prioritize well-being by acknowledging sense-making processes, being descriptive about their own experiences, and modeling curiosity about others' perspectives. This helps clear up misinterpretations and faulty assumptions that can lead to dysfunctional organizations. By creating space for educators to share their experiences, principals foster more accurate understandings and collaborative relationships.

Action Over Avoidance (Chapter 7)

By *embedding reflection into teachers' daily routines*, school leaders can overcome *avoidance* as an enemy of efficacy.

Posing Reflective Questions

Principals can use open-ended, reflective questioning to facilitate evidence-based discussions among teacher teams. By posing questions that link outcomes with efforts, foster perspective taking, probe for deeper understanding, prompt action, and promote conceptual understanding, principals encourage teachers to critically analyze their practice, reflect on biases, and transform insights into concrete actions that improve student learning. Inviting participation from all team members is crucial.

Modeling Evidence-Based Reflection

Principals can model evidence-based reflection by presenting and analyzing schoolwide data, publicly reflecting on implications, and engaging teachers in data-based discussions. Connecting data to goals and sharing examples of data-informed decisions help create a culture where teachers habitually use data to inform their own reflections and decisions rather than rely on assumptions.

Guiding Strengths-Based Approaches

Reflective practices build collective efficacy, but self-critical reflection can undermine it. Leaders can guide teachers toward strengths-based reflection, focusing on successes and positive qualities rather than deficits. Methods include identifying strengths, reflecting by journaling, setting strengths-based goals, and holding peer support groups. By cultivating a strengths-based mindset, principals enhance teachers' self-awareness, resilience, and well-being, ultimately contributing to collective efficacy.

Criteria Over Comparison (Chapter 8)

By *measuring progress against a predetermined criterion*, school leaders can overcome *comparison* as an enemy of efficacy.

Setting Mastery Goals

Leaders can help teams set mastery goals by focusing on progress and asking, "What does the team want to get better at regarding student outcomes?" Principals can encourage teachers to think about skills and standards and help to ensure the goal is something that teachers can impact through their efforts.

Identifying Criterion-Based Success

Leaders can help teams determine success criteria based on identified student learning needs and an identified teacher learning need. Principals can help teachers identify success criteria by co-constructing it together and asking, "If we were to be successful with [insert target], what would that look like?"

Providing Goal-Referenced Feedback

Goal-referenced feedback is specific, relevant, timeless, evidence-based, and actionable. In relation to the goal set by the team, principals provide clear and concrete suggestions for improvement or next steps that teams can take to move closer to achieving their goals.

Empowerment Over Hierarchy (Chapter 9)

By *developing teacher leaders*, school leaders can overcome *hierarchy* as an enemy of efficacy.

Validating Informal Leadership

Principals can validate informal teacher leadership by recognizing and appreciating the daily contributions teachers make, such as sharing strategies, upholding standards, and advocating for students. By acknowledging leadership efforts, providing resources and opportunities, and showcasing examples, principals create a culture of shared leadership where all educators feel empowered to make a meaningful impact on student learning and school success.

Expanding Opportunities for Formal Leadership

Principals can expand formal teacher leadership opportunities by creating new roles or revising existing ones based on the school's needs. Such roles include data coach, equity champion, or technology specialist. Establishing a leadership pipeline with a clear pathway from informal to formal roles, providing support and mentoring, and developing succession plans empower teacher leaders and foster collective efficacy for improved student outcomes.

Increasing Teacher Autonomy and Decision Making

Increasing teacher autonomy and decision-making power within a framework of collective interdependence and accountability can lead to greater engagement, creativity, and performance. By allowing teachers to make instructional decisions, pursue professional learning, and collaborate with colleagues, principals empower them to take ownership of their practice and generate solutions that positively impact student outcomes. Striking the right balance and providing support are key to realizing the benefits of teacher autonomy.

Interdependence Over Isolation (Chapter 10)

By *increasing interdependencies*, school leaders can overcome *isolation* as an enemy of efficacy.

Extending Invitations to Say More

A simple strategy principals can use to develop rich conversations is to extend an invitation for teachers to say more. Rather than stopping at reassurance or moving quickly to a remedy, teachers are more likely to unpack the nature of the problem when they are invited to say more, and the conversation yields more than a quick fix.

Helping Teams Set Interdependent Goals

School leaders can organize structured goal-setting sessions where teachers work in grade-level or subject-area teams to develop interdependent goals. Interdependent goals imply collective action and shared responsibility. School leaders can dedicate regular time for teacher teams to meet, discuss progress toward their goals, share best practices, and brainstorm strategies to overcome challenges.

Engaging Teams in Interdependent Tasks

Task interdependence refers to how well connected teachers are based on the tasks they engage in while working collaboratively. Leaders can structure tasks that require greater interdependence by providing opportunities for teachers to plan, deliver, and debrief lessons based on identified student learning needs.

Consensus Over Ambiguity (Chapter 11)

By *building consensus*, school leaders can overcome *ambiguity* as an enemy of efficacy.

Guiding an Affinity-Mapping Process

Principals can guide affinity mapping to help teachers organize ideas, find common ground, and build consensus. The process involves brainstorming ideas, silently grouping related notes, naming themes, and discussing insights. Affinity mapping can be used for analyzing data, planning curriculum, solving problems, reflecting on practices, and developing initiatives. By ensuring equal contributions and reducing power dynamics, affinity mapping fosters inclusive collaboration and shared understanding.

Using the Realm of Concern Versus Realm of Influence Protocol

The realm of concern and realm of influence protocol helps teachers focus on areas they can directly impact. Principals lead the process by having teachers brainstorm concerns, categorize them as within their influence or concern, brainstorm actions for concerns within their influence, prioritize actions, and develop an action plan. This collaborative process builds consensus, ownership, and collective efficacy in addressing challenges and improving student outcomes.

Analyzing Student Work Samples

Analyzing student work samples is a powerful way to build consensus among teachers. By examining student artifacts, teachers can identify strengths, anticipate challenges, and strategize adjustments to their teaching approaches. This open dialogue allows for clarifying misconceptions, sharing ideas and strategies, and mapping out next steps. The process fosters shared understanding, commitment, and action, ultimately improving student outcomes.

Focus Over Fragmentation (Chapter 12)

By *focusing on implementation*, school leaders can overcome *fragmentation* as an enemy of efficacy.

Gatekeeping

Practicing gatekeeping is fairly simple. After educators have identified one or two priorities, they should consistently ask the question "Will it improve students' [insert priority here]?" when considering any new idea, initiative, or program. If the answer is *no*, they shouldn't let it through the gate.

Applying the 80/20 Principle

System and school leaders can apply the 80/20 principle by identifying the 20 percent of things that are likely causing 80 percent of the outcomes and then determining how to reduce or eliminate the actions and activities that are not impactful. The 80/20 principle is about helping to identify and focus only on the things that will deeply enhance student outcomes.

Prioritizing Evidence-Based Strategies

Leaders can ensure that evidence-based practices are implemented by concentrating publicly and persistently on improving the quality of classroom instruction. By engaging teachers and teams in reviewing their fidelity in utilizing the strategies, and then using this information to determine what further implementation supports teachers need, principals prioritize evidence-based strategies.

References and Resources

Adams, C. M., & Forsyth, P. B. (2006). Proximate sources of collective teacher efficacy. *Journal of Educational Administration, 44*(6), 625–642.

Akkuzu, N. (2014). The role of different types of feedback in the reciprocal interaction of teaching performance and self-efficacy belief. *Australian Journal of Teacher Education, 39*(3), 37–66.

Allen, C. D., & Penuel, W. R. (2015). Studying teachers' sensemaking to investigate teachers' responses to professional development focused on new standards. *Journal of Teacher Education, 66*(2), 136–149.

Anderson, C. M. (2022). *Leading a narrative of collective efficacy*. Accessed at https://issuu.com/ilascdpublishing/docs/february_2022_journal/s/14874463 on June 27, 2024.

Aritzeta, A., & Balluerka, N. (2006). Cooperation, competition, and goal interdependence in work teams: A multilevel approach. *Psicothema, 18*(4), 757–765.

Arzonetti Hite, S., & Donohoo, J. (2021). *Leading collective efficacy: Powerful stories of achievement and equity*. Thousand Oaks, CA: Corwin.

Australian Institute for Teaching and School Leadership. (2012). *Australian teacher performance and development framework*. Melbourne, Victoria, Australia: Author.

Bandura, A. (1977). Self-efficacy: Toward a unifying theory of behavioral change. *Psychological Review, 84*(2), 191–215.

Bandura, A. (1982). Self-efficacy mechanism in human agency. *American Psychologist, 37*(2), 122–147.

Bandura, A. (1993). Perceived self-efficacy in cognitive development and functioning. *Educational Psychologist, 28*(2): 117–148.

Bandura, A. (1997). *Self-efficacy: The exercise of control*. New York: W. H. Freeman and Company.

Bandura, A. (1998). Personal and collective efficacy in personal adaptation and change. In J. G. Adair, D. Belanger, & K. L. Dion (Eds), *Advances in psychological science, Volume 1* (pp. 51–71). London: Psychology Press.

Bandura, A. (2000). Exercise of human agency through collective efficacy. *Current Directions in Psychological Science, 9*(3), 75–78.

Bandura, A. (2006). Toward a psychology of human agency. *Perspectives on Psychological Science, 1*(2), 164–180.

Bandura, A., & Jourden, F. J. (1991). Self-regulatory mechanisms governing the impact of social comparison on complex decision making. *Journal of Personality and Social Psychology, 60*(6), 941–951.

Baumeister, R., Bratslavsky, E., Finkenauer, C., & de Vohs, K. (2001). Bad is stronger than good. *Review of General Psychology, 5*(4), 323–370.

Beare, H. (2001). *Creating the future school.* New York: Routledge.

Beauchamp, L., Klassen, R., Parsons, J., Durksen, T., & Taylor, L. (2014). *Exploring the development of teacher efficacy through professional learning experiences.* Edmonton, Alberta, Canada: Alberta Teachers' Association.

Bennett, N., & Lemoine, G. J. (2014). What a difference a work makes: Understanding threats to performance in a VUCA world. *Business Horizons, 57*(3), 311–317.

Berg, J. H. (2018). Leading together: Educating ourselves for equity. *Educational Leadership, 76*(3), 84–85.

Berger, J. (2020). *The catalyst: How to change anyone's mind.* New York: Simon & Schuster.

Bottiani, J. H., Duran, C. A. K., Pas, E. T., & Bradshaw, C. P. (2019). Teacher stress and burnout in urban middle schools: Associations with job demands, resources, and effective classroom practices. *Journal of School Psychology, 77*, 36–51.

Bradt, G. (2023). *Simplify planning so all can COPE: Context, objectives, priorities, enablers*. Forbes. Accessed at www.forbes.com/sites/georgebradt/2023/02/14/simplify-planning-so-all-can-cope-context-objectives-priorities-enablers/?sh=51d7a36f336b on June 27, 2024.

Breakspear, S., & Rosenbrock, M. (2024). *The pruning principle: Mastering the art of strategic subtraction within education.* Melbourne: Amba Press.

Bryk, A. S., Easton, J. Q., Kerbow, D., Rollow, S. G., & Bender Sebring, P. (1993). *A view from the elementary schools: The state of reform in Chicago*. Accessed at https://consortium.uchicago.edu/publications/view-elementary-schools-state-reform-chicago on June 27, 2024.

Bschor, T., Negel, L., Unger, J. Schwarzer, G., Baethge, C. (2024). Differential outcomes of placebo treatment across 9 psychiatric disorders: A systematic review and meta-analysis. *JAMA Psychiatry, 81*(8), 757–768.

Buckingham, M., & Goodall, A. (2019). *The feedback fallacy*. Boston: Harvard Business.

Burke, C. J. F., & Adler, M. (2013). Personal consequences of compliance and resistance to mandated reforms for teachers in low-performing schools. *Journal of Urban Learning, Teaching, & Research, 9*, 6–17.

Bushe, G. R. (2010). *Clear leadership: Sustaining real collaboration and partnership at work*. Boston: Davies-Black.

Butler, R. (1987). Task-involving and ego-involving properties of evaluation: Effects of different feedback conditions on motivational perceptions, interest and performance. *Journal of Educational Psychology, 79*(4), 474–482.

Cantrell, S. C., & Callaway, P. (2008). High and low implementers of content literacy instruction: Portraits of teacher efficacy. *Teaching and Teacher Education, 24*(7), 1739–1750.

Capel, S. A., Sisley, B. L., & Desertrain, G. S. (2009). The relationship of role conflict and role ambiguity to burnout in high school basketball coaches. *Journal of Sport and Exercise Psychology*, *9*(2), 106–117.

Caprara, G. V., Barbaranelli, C., Borgogni, L., & Steca, P. (2003). Efficacy beliefs as determinants of teachers' job satisfaction. *Journal of Educational Psychology*, *95*(4), 821–832.

Cassata, A., & Allensworth, E. (2021). Scaling standards-aligned instruction through teacher leadership: Methods, supports, and challenges. *International Journal of STEM Education*, *8*, Article 39.

Çelik, K. (2013). The effect of role ambiguity and role conflict on performance of vice principal: The mediating role of burnout. *Eurasian Journal of Education Research*, *51*, 195–214.

Clark, T. R. (2020). *The 4 stages of psychological safety: Defining the path to inclusion*. Oakland, CA: Berrett-Koehler.

Cohen-Zamir, A., & Vedder-Weiss, D. (2024). Blame avoidance and facework in teachers' collaborative decision-making. *Teachers and Teaching: Theory and Practice*, *30*(1), 85–101.

Conzemius, A. E., & O'Neill, J. (2014). *The handbook for SMART school teams: Revitalizing best practices for collaboration* (2nd ed.). Bloomington, IN: Solution Tree Press.

Coutifaris, C. G. V., & Grant, A. M. (2022) Taking your team behind the curtain: The effects of leader feedback-sharing and feedback-seeking on team psychological safety. *Organization Science*, *33*(4), 1574–1598.

Crow, T. (2008). Declaration of interdependence. Q & A with Judith Warren Little. *Journal of Staff Development*, *29*(3), 53–56.

Culbreth, J. R., Scarborough, J. L., Banks-Johnson, A., & Solomon, S. (2005). Role stress among practicing school counselors. *Counselor Education and Supervision*, *45*(1), 58–71.

Derrington, M. L., & Angelle, P. S. (2013). Teacher leadership and collective efficacy: Connections and links. *International Journal of Teacher Leadership*, *4*(1), 1–13.

DeWitt, P. M. (2022). *De-implementation: Creating the space to focus on what works*. Thousand Oaks, CA: Corwin.

Donohoo, J., & Anderson, C. (2022). Designing the collaboration of tomorrow. *Principals' Connections*, *25*(3).

Donohoo, J., Bryen, S., & Weishar, B. (2018). Implementing high-leverage influences from the Visible Learning Synthesis: Six supporting conditions. *Education Science*, *8*, 2015.

Donohoo, J., Hattie, J., & Eells, R. (2018). The power of collective efficacy. *Educational Leadership*, *75*(6), 40–44.

Donohoo, J., & Katz, S. (2020). *Quality implementation: Leveraging collective efficacy to make "what works" actually work*. Thousand Oaks, CA: Corwin.

Donohoo, J., O'Leary, T., & Hattie, J. (2020). The design and validation of the enabling conditions for collective teacher efficacy scale (EC-CTES). *The Journal of Professional Capital and Community*, *5*(2), 147–166.

Donohoo, J., & Velasco, M. (2016). *The transformative power of collaborative inquiry: Realizing change in schools and classrooms*. Thousand Oaks, CA: Corwin.

Duhigg, C. (2014). *The power of habit: Why we do what we do in life and business*. New York: Random House.

Duhigg, C. (2016). What Google learned from its quest to build the perfect team. *The New York Times Magazine*. Accessed at www.nytimes.com/2016/02/28/magazine/what-google-learned-from-its-quest-to-build-the-perfect-team.html on June 27, 2024.

Dweck, C. S. (1975). The role of expectations and attributions in the alleviation of learned helplessness. *Journal of Personality and Social Psychology*, *31*(4), 674–685.

Dweck, C. S. (2006). *Mindset: The new psychology of success*. New York: Random House.

Dweck, C. S. (2017). *Mindset: Changing the way you think to fulfill your potential* (Updated ed.). New York: Little, Brown.

Earl, L. M., & Katz, S. (2006). *Leading schools in a data-rich world: Harnessing data for school improvement*. Thousand Oaks, CA: Corwin.

Edmondson, A. C. (2019). *The fearless organization: Creating psychological safety in the workplace for learning, innovation, and growth*. Hoboken, NJ: Wiley.

Eells, R. J. (2011). *Meta-analysis of the relationship between collective teacher efficacy and student achievement* [Doctoral dissertation, Loyola University of Chicago]. Loyola eCommons. Accessed at https://ecommons.luc.edu/luc_diss/133/ on October 12, 2024.

Elliott, K., & Hollingsworth, H. (2020). *A case for reimagining school leadership development to enhance collective efficacy*. Camberwell, Victoria, Australia: Australian Council for Educational Research.

Ellsberg, D. (1961). Risk, ambiguity, and the savage axioms. *The Quarterly Journal of Economics*, *75*(4), 643–669.

Elmore, R. F. (2000). *Building a new structure for school leadership*. Washington, DC: The Albert Shanker Institute.

Ertmer, P. A., Ottenbreit-Leftwich, A. T., Sadik, O., Sendurur, E., & Sendurur, P. (2012). Teacher beliefs and technology integration practices: A critical relationship. *Computers & Education*, *59*(2), 423–435.

Evans, A. (2009). No child left behind and the quest for educational equity: The role of teachers' collective sense of efficacy. *Leadership and Policy in Schools*, *8*, 64–91.

Ferguson, K. (2023). *Head & heart: The art of modern leadership*. Oakland, CA: Berrett-Koehler.

Festinger, L. (1954). A theory of social comparison processes. *Human Relations*, *7*(2), 117–140.

Flinders, D. J. (2019). The problems of isolation and the promise of connectivity: New research on the emergence of teacher isolation in the United States. In A. Sullivan, B. Johnson, & M. Simons (Eds.), *Attracting and keeping the best teachers: Issues and opportunities* (pp. 71–90). New York: Springer.

Forte, A. M., & Flores, M. A. (2014). Teacher collaboration and professional development in the workplace: A study of Portuguese teachers. *European Journal of Teacher Education*, *37*(1), 91–105.

Fredrickson, B. L. (2001). The role of positive emotions in positive psychology: The broaden-and-build theory of positive emotions. *American Psychologist*, *56*(3), 218–226.

Fullan, M., & Hargreaves, A. (2016). *Bringing the profession back in: Call to action.* Accessed at https://michaelfullan.ca/wp-content/uploads/2017/11/16_BringingProfessionFullanHargreaves2016.pdf on June 27, 2024.

Fullan, M., & Quinn, J. (2016). *Coherence: The right drivers in action for schools, districts, and systems.* Thousand Oaks, CA: Corwin.

Gibbs, S., & Powell, B. (2012). Teacher efficacy and pupil behavior: The structure of teachers' individual and collective beliefs and their relationship with numbers of pupils excluded from school. *British Journal of Educational Psychology, 82*(4), 564–584.

Gladwell, M. (2008). *Outliers: The story of success.* New York: Little, Brown.

Guskey, T. R. (1987). Context variables that affect measures of teacher efficacy. *The Journal of Educational Research, 81*(1), 41–47.

Goddard, R. D. (2002). Collective efficacy and school organization: A multilevel analysis of influence in schools. *Theory and Research in Educational Administration, 1*, 169–184.

Goddard, R. D., & Goddard, Y. L. (2001). A multilevel analysis of the relationship between teacher and collective efficacy in urban schools. *Teaching and Teacher Education, 17*(7), 807–818.

Goddard, R. D., Goddard, Y. L., Kim, E. S., & Miller, R. (2015). A theoretical and empirical analysis of the roles of instructional leadership, teacher collaboration, and collective beliefs in support of student learning. *American Journal of Education, 121*(4), 501–530.

Goddard, R. D., Hoy, W. K, & Hoy, A. W. (2000). Collective teacher efficacy: Its meaning, measure, and impact on student achievement. *American Educational Research Journal, 37*(2), 479–507.

Goddard, R. D., Skrla, L., & Salloum, S. J. (2017). The role of collective efficacy in closing student achievement gaps: A mixed methods study of school leadership for excellence and equity. *Journal of Education for Students Placed at Risk, 22*(4), 1–17.

Green, A. (2022). *Teacher wellbeing: A real conversation for teachers and leaders.* Melbourne, Victoria, Australia: Amba Press.

Grupe, D. W., & Nitschke, J. B. (2013). Uncertainty and anticipation in anxiety: An integrated neurobiological and psychological perspective. *Nature Reviews Neuroscience, 14*, 488–501.

Gulati, R., Casto, C., & Krontiris, C. (2014). How the other Fukushima plant survived. *Harvard Business Review.* Accessed at https://hbr.org/2014/07/how-the-other-fukushima-plant-survived on June 26, 2024.

Gully, S. M., Incalcaterra, K. A., Joshi, A., & Beauien, J. M. (2002). A meta-analysis of team-efficacy, potency, and performance: Interdependence and level of analysis as moderators of observed relationships. *Journal of Applied Psychology, 87*(5), 819–832.

Hall, G. E., & Hord, S. M. (2006). *Implementing change: Patterns, principles, and potholes* (2nd ed.). Boston: Pearson.

Hall, G. E., & Hord, S. M. (2015). *Implementing change: Patterns, principles, and potholes* (4th ed.). Boston: Pearson.

Hallinger, P. (2003). Leading educational change: Reflections on the practice of instructional and transformational leadership. *Cambridge Journal of Education, 33*(3), 329–352.

Hameleers, M. (2021). Prospect theory in times of a pandemic: The effects of gain versus loss framing on risky choices and emotional responses during the 2020 coronavirus outbreak. *Mass Communication and Society*, *24*(4), 479–499.

Hamilton, A., Hattie, J., & Wiliam, D. (2023). *Making room for impact: A de-implementation guide for educators*. Thousand Oaks, CA: Corwin.

Hanover Research. (2022*). Facilitating conversations for consensus: Prepared for the Virginia Department of Education*. Accessed at https://content.govdelivery.com/attachments/VADOE/2022/02/09/file_attachments/2072320/VDOE%20-%20February%202022%20Bulletin.pdf on October 12, 2024.

Hargreaves, A., & Fullan, M. (2012). *Professional capital: Transforming teaching in every school.* New York: Teachers College Press.

Harrison, C., & Killion, J. (2007). Ten roles for teacher leaders. *Educational Leadership*, *65*(1), 74–77.

Hattie, J. (2023). *Visible learning: The sequel—A synthesis of over 2,100 meta-analyses relating to achievement*. New York: Routledge.

Heath, C., & Heath, D. (2017). *The power of moments: Why certain experiences have extraordinary impact*. New York: Simon & Schuster.

Herman, K. C., Hickmon-Rosa, J., & Reinke, W. M. (2018). Empirically derived profiles of teacher stress, burnout, self-efficacy, and coping and associated student outcomes. *Journal of Positive Behavior Interventions*, *20*(2), 90–100.

Hogg, M. A. (2000). Social identity and social comparison. In J. Suls & L. Wheeler (Eds.), *Handbook of social comparison: Theory and research* (pp. 401–421). Dordrecht, Netherlands: Kluwer Academic Publishers.

Hoy, W. K., Sweetland, S. R., & Smith, P. A. (2002). Toward an organizational model of achievement in high schools: The significance of collective efficacy. *Educational Administration Quarterly*, *38*(1), 77–93.

Hoy, W. K., Tarter, C. J., & Hoy, A. W. (2006). Academic optimism of schools: A force for student achievement. *American Educational Research Journal*, *43*(3), 425–446.

Inbar-Furst, H., & Gumpel, T. P. (2015). Factors affecting female teachers' attitudes toward help-seeking or help-avoidance in coping with behavioral problems. *Psychology in the Schools*, *52*(9), 906–922.

Ingersoll, R. M. (2007). Short on power, long on responsibility. *Educational Leadership*, *65*(1), 20–25.

Jackson, T. (2023). *Five approaches for changing a hierarchical command-and-control organization*. Forbes. Accessed at www.forbes.com/sites/forbescoachescouncil/2023/01/10/five-approaches-for-changing-a-hierarchical-command-and-control-organization on June 26, 2024.

Katz, S. (2015). *What are we learning about supervisory officer learning*? Accessed at https://opsoa.org/application/files/2014/8476/1200/SO_Learning_Monograph_16–04.pdf on June 26, 2024.

Katz, S., & Dack, L. A. (2013). *Intentional interruption: Breaking down learning barriers to transform professional practice*. Thousand Oaks, CA: Corwin.

Katz-Navon, T., & Erez, M. (2005). When collective- and self-efficacy affect team performance: The role of task interdependence. *Small Group Research*, *36*(4), 437–465.

Keil, F. C. (2006). Explanation and understanding. *Annual Review of Psychology, 57,* 227–254.

Kim, S.-i., Lee, M.-J., Chung, Y., & Bong, M. (2010). Comparison of brain activation during norm-referenced versus criterion-referenced feedback: The role of perceived competence and performance-approach goals. *Contemporary Educational Psychology, 35*(2), 141–152.

Kirschner, P. A., Sweller, J., Kirschner, F., & Zambrano, J. (2018). From cognitive load theory to collaborative cognitive load theory. *International Journal of Computer-Supported Collaborative Learning, 13,* 213–233.

Klassen, R. M., Usher, E. L., & Bong, M. (2010). Teachers' collective efficacy, job satisfaction, and job stress in cross-cultural context. *The Journal of Experimental Education, 78*(4), 464–486.

Kleinhans, R., & Bolt. G. (2013). More than just fear: On the intricate interplay between perceived neighborhood disorder, collective efficacy, and action. *Journal of Urban Affairs, 36*(3), 1–47.

Kurz, T. B., & Knight, S. L. (2004). An exploration of the relationship among teacher efficacy, collective teacher efficacy, and goal consensus. *Learning Environments Research, 7*(2), 111–128.

Laposa, J. M., Katz, D. E., Lisi, D. M., Hawley, L. L., Quigley, L., & Rector, N. A. (2022). Longitudinal changes in intolerance of uncertainty and worry severity during CBT for generalized anxiety disorder. *Journal of Anxiety Disorders, 91,* 102606.

Lee, V. E., Dedrick, R. F., & Smith, J. B. (1991). The effect of the social organization of schools on teachers' efficacy and satisfaction. *Sociology of Education, 64*(3), 190–208.

Leithwood, K., Harris, A., & Hopkins, D. (2008). Seven strong claims about successful school leadership. *School Leadership & Management, 28*(1), 27–42.

Leithwood, K., Louis, K. S., Anderson, S., & Wahlstrom, K. (2004). *How leadership influences student learning.* Wallace. Accessed at https://wallacefoundation.org/report/how-leadership-influences-student-learning on June 26, 2024.

Lieberman, A., & Miller, L. (2004). *Teacher leadership.* San Francisco: Jossey-Bass.

Lieberman, A., & Miller, L. (2005). Teachers as leaders. *The Educational Forum, 69,* 151–162.

Lindsley, D. H., Brass, D. J., & Thomas, J. B. (1995). Efficacy-performance spirals: A multilevel perspective. *The Academy of Management Review, 20*(3), 645–678.

Little, J. W. (1990). The persistence of privacy: Autonomy and initiative in teachers' professional relations. *Teachers College Record, 91*(4), 509–536.

Lortie, D. C. (1975). *Schoolteacher: A sociological study.* Chicago: University of Chicago Press.

Macovei, C. M., Bumbuc, S., & Martinescu-Bădălan, F. (2023). Personality traits, role ambiguity, and relational competence as predictors for teacher subjective wellbeing. *Secondary Educational Psychology, 13,* 101470.

Madden, J. (2017). *A practical guide for consensus-based decision making.* Accessed at https://www.tamarackcommunity.ca/hubfs/Resources/Tools/Practical%20Guide%20for%20Consensus-Based%20Decision%20Making.pdf on October 12, 2024.

Martinez, A., & Huber, T. (2019). Attributional feedback and its effect on self-beliefs and academic achievement: A review of the literature. *International Journal of Current Research, 11*(3), 2242–2246.

Marzano, R. J. (2012). Art and science of teaching: It's how you use a strategy. *Educational Leadership, 69*(4), 88–89.

Marzano, R. J. (2017). *The new art and science of teaching*. Bloomington, IN: Solution Tree Press.

Marzano, R. J., Waters, T., & McNulty, B. A. (2005). *School leadership that works: From research to results*. Arlington, VA: ASCD.

Morris-Rothschild, B. K., & Brassard, M. R. (2006). Teachers' conflict management styles: The role of attachment styles and classroom management efficacy. *Journal of School Psychology, 44*(2), 105–121.

Morriss, J., Goh, K., Hirsch, C. R., & Dodd, H. F. (2023). Intolerance of uncertainty heightens negative emotional states and dampens positive emotional states. *Frontiers in Psychiatry*, 1–9.

National School Reform Faculty. (n.d.a). *NSRF protocols and activities. . . from A to Z*. Accessed at https://nsrfharmony.org/protocols on June 26, 2024.

National School Reform Faculty. (n.d.b). *Realms of concern and influence*. Accessed at www.nsrfharmony.org/wp-content/uploads/2017/10/realms_concern _influence_0.pdf on September 3, 2024.

Norris, R. J., & Mullinix, K. J. (2020). Framing innocence: An experimental test of the effects of wrongful convictions on public opinion. *Journal of Experimental Criminology, 16*(2), 311–334.

Ostovar-Nameghi, S. A., & Sheikhahmadi, M. (2016). From teacher isolation to teacher collaboration: Theoretical perspectives and empirical findings. *English Language Teaching, 9*(5), 197–205.

Parker, L. E. (1994). Working together: Perceived self- and collective-efficacy at the workplace. *Journal of Applied Social Psychology, 24*(1), 43–59.

Parks, M., Solmon, M., & Lee, A. (2007). Understanding classroom teachers' perceptions of integrating physical activity: A collective efficacy perspective. *Journal of Research in Childhood Education, 21*(3), 316–328.

Pink, D. H. (2009). *Drive: The surprising truth about what motivates us.* New York: Riverhead Books.

Pizarro Milian, R., Reynolds, D., Naleni, J., Firrisaa, A., Parekh, G., Brown, R., et al. (2024). Pathways to success, or unfulfilled dreams? An examination of pathway-based disparities in graduation rates. *Journal of College Student Retention: Research, Theory & Practice*. Article 10.1177/15210251231220869.

Prelli, G. E. (2016). How school leaders might promote higher levels of collective teacher efficacy at the level of school and team. *English Language Teaching*, 9(3), 174–180. https://doi.org/10.5539/elt.v9n3p174

Prilop, C. N., Weber, K. E., Prins, F. J., & Kleinknecht, M. (2021). Connecting feedback to self-efficacy: Receiving and providing peer feedback in teacher education. *Studies in Educational Evaluation, 70*(2), 101058.

Qadach, M., Schechter, C., & Da'as, R. (2020). Instructional leadership and teachers' intent to leave: The mediating role of collective teacher efficacy and shared vision. *Educational Management Administration & Leadership, 48*(4), 617–634.

Qianggiang, M. (2021). The role of teacher autonomy support on students' academic engagement and resilience. *Frontiers in Psychology, 12*. https://doi.org/10.3389/fpsyg.2021.778581

Qu, H., & Daniel, J. L. (2020). Is "overhead" a tainted word? A survey experiment exploring framing effects of nonprofit overhead on donor decisions. *Nonprofit and Voluntary Sector Quarterly, 50*(2), 397–419.

Quintero, S., & Long, J. (n.d.). Toxic positivity: The dark side of positive vibes [Blog post]. *The Psychology Group*. Accessed at https://thepsychologygroup.com/toxic-positivity on June 26, 2024.

Ramos, M. F. H., Silva, S. S. C., Pontes, F. A. R., Fernandez, A. P. O., & Nina, K. C. F. (2014). Collective teacher efficacy beliefs: A critical review of the literature. *International Journal of Humanities and Social Science, 4*(7), 179–188.

Ravishankar, R. A. (2022). A guide to building psychological safety on your team. *Harvard Business Review*. Accessed at https://hbr.org/2022/12/a-guide-to-building-psychological-safety-on-your-team on June 26, 2024.

Reese, S. D., Gandy, O. H., Jr., & Grant, A. E. (2001). *Framing public life: Perspectives on media and our understanding of the social world*. Mahwah, NJ: Erlbaum.

Reeves, D. B. (2008). *Reframing teacher leadership to improve your school*. Arlington, VA: ASCD.

Robinson, V. M. J., Lloyd, C. A., & Rowe, K. J. (2008). The impact of leadership on student outcomes: An analysis of the differential effects of leadership types. *Educational Administration Quarterly, 44*(5), 635–674.

Ross, J. A., Hogaboam-Gray, A., & Gray, P. (2004). Prior student achievement, collaborative school processes, and collective teacher efficacy. *Leadership and Policy in Schools, 3*(3), 163–188.

Salloum, S. J. (2021). Building coherence: An investigation of collective efficacy, social context, and how leaders shape teachers' work. *American Journal of Education, 128*(2), 203–243.

Sandoval, J. M., Challoo, L., & Kupczynski, L. (2011). The relationship between teachers' collective efficacy and student achievement at economically disadvantaged middle school campus. *Journal of Educational Psychology, 5*(1), 9–23.

Schechter, C., & Qadach, M. (2012). Toward an organizational model of change in elementary schools: The contribution of organizational learning mechanisms. *Educational Administration Quarterly, 48*(1), 116–153.

Schlichte, J., Yssel, N., & Merbler, J. (2005). Pathways to burnout: Case studies in teacher isolation and alienation. *Preventing School Failure: Alternative Education for Children and Youth, 50*(1), 35–40.

Schmoker, M. (2011). *Focus: Elevating the essentials to radically improve student learning*. Arlington, VA: ASCD.

Schunk, D. (2003). Try harder? Motivational effects of effort attributional feedback. *Eric Digest*. Accessed at https://files.eric.ed.gov/fulltext/ED479353.pdf on June 26, 2024.

Seijts, G., & Latham, G. P. (2005). Learning versus performance goals: When should each be used? *Academy of Management Perspectives, 19*(1), 124–131.

Sparks, D. (2007). *Leading for results: Transforming teaching, learning, and relationships in schools* (2nd ed.). Thousand Oaks, CA: Corwin.

Spillane, J. P., & Diamond, J. B. (2007). *Distributed leadership in practice.* New York: Teachers College Press.

Stricker, J. (2019). Bringing intentionality to instructional leadership teams. *Educational Leadership, 76*(9). Accessed at https://ascd.org/el/articles/bringing-intentionality-to-instructional-leadership-teams on September 25, 2024.

Stone, D., & David-Lang, J. (2017). Stop sabotaging feedback. *Educational Leadership, 74*(8), 47–50.

Timperley, H., & Robinson, V. (2000). Workload and professional culture of teachers. *Educational Management & Administration, 28*(1), 47–62.

Tschannen-Moran, M. (2001). The effects of a state-wide conflict management initiative in schools. *American Secondary Education, 29*(3), 2–32.

Tschannen-Moran, M., & Barr, M. (2004). Fostering student learning: The relationship of collective teacher efficacy and student achievement. *Leadership and Policy in Schools, 3*(3), 189–209.

USBE Teaching and Learning. (June 30, 2023). *Collaborative teams making impact* (Drafted by JT) [Video]. YouTube. www.youtube.com/watch?v=THvUI1p65to&list=PLtk_b3zV7zIsygOqbjKU_quBmlbnbrTzK&index=6

van Kleef, G. A., & Côté, S. (2022). The social effects of emotions. *Annual Review of Psychology, 73*, 629–658.

Vanlommel, K., van den Boom-Muilenburg, S. N., Thesingh, J., & Kikken, È. (2023). How a sense of collective efficacy influences teacher learning during change: The role of academic optimism and shared vision. *Journal of Professional Capital and Community, 8*(1), 1–16.

Voss, C. (2017). *Never split the difference: Negotiating as if your life depended on it.* New York: Random House.

Walker, A. R., Navarro, D. J., Newell, B. R., & Beesley, T. (2022). Protection from uncertainty in the exploration/exploitation trade-off. *Journal of Experimental Psychology: Learning, Memory, and Cognition, 48*(4), 547–568.

Waltré, E., Dietz, B., & van Knippenberg, D. (2023). Leadership shaping social comparison to improve performance: A field experiment. *The Leadership Quarterly, 34*(5), 1–19.

Wheatley, M. J. (2002). *Turning to one another: Simple conversations to restore hope to the future.* Oakland, CA: BerrettKoehler.

Wisniewski, B., Zierer, K., & Hattie, J. (2020). The power of feedback revisited: A Meta analysis of educational feedback research. *Frontiers in Psychology, 10.* https://doi.org/10.3389/fpsyg.2019.03087

York-Barr, J., & Duke, K. (2004). What do we know about teacher leadership? Findings from two decades of scholarship. *Review of Educational Research, 74*(3), 255–316.

York-Barr, J., Sommers, W. A., Ghere, G. S., & Montie, J. (2006). *Reflective practice to improve schools: An action guide for educators* (2nd ed.). Thousand Oaks, CA: Corwin.

Yurt, E. (2022). Collective teacher self-efficacy and burnout: The mediator role of job satisfaction. *International Journal of Modern Education Studies, 6*(1), 51–69.

Index

J

K

L

M

N

O

P

S

Y

Z

Harnessing the Power of Collective Teacher Efficacy
Jamie Virga
Build the collective efficacy of teacher teams through the five-step research-supported process of CLEAR: clarify, listen, explore, activate, and review. This practical guidebook helps leaders and coaches build collective teacher efficacy through powerful scenarios, practical steps, and user-friendly tools.
BKG175

Ensuring Teachers Matter
Shelly Wilfong and Ryan Donlan
Teachers are critical to student success, but the profession is in crisis. Drawing from original research, this practical resource introduces eight essential elements that schools need to have for teachers to feel they matter.
BKG111

Teacher Leaders, Classroom Champions
Jeanetta Jones Miller
Gain a clear path to activate school improvement from within your classroom. This book shares a vision of teacher leadership not as teachers who lead other teachers but as those who take responsibility in supporting other teachers, students, and families in a variety of ways.
BKG110

Collective Efficacy in a PLC at Work®
Matt Navo and Jared J. Savage
How did one of California's lowest-performing districts become a top turnaround district? It all came down to building collective team efficacy. Dive into this resource to find parallels to your own story and apply the lessons learned at Sanger Unified to the school community you serve.
BKF973

Solution Tree | Press 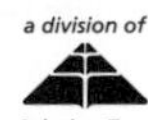

Visit SolutionTree.com or call 800.733.6786 to order.